AAT

Qualification

AQ2013

LEVEL 4 DIF

(QCF)

QUESTION

First edition June 2013
ISBN 9781 4727 0357 6

British Library Cataloguing-in-Publication Data
A catalogue record for this book is available from the British Library

Published by
BPP Learning Media Ltd
BPP House
Aldine Place
London W12 8AA

www.bpp.com/learningmedia

Printed in the United Kingdom by Martins of Berwick
Sea View Works
Spittal
Berwick-Upon-Tweed
TD15 1RS

Your learning materials, published by BPP Learning Media Ltd, are printed on paper obtained from traceable sustainable sources.

CONTENTS

A NOTE ABOUT COPYRIGHT

Dear Customer

What does the little © mean and why does it matter?

Your market-leading BPP books, course materials and e-learning materials do not write and update themselves. People write them: on their own behalf or as employees of an organisation that invests in this activity. Copyright law protects their livelihoods. It does so by creating rights over the use of the content.

Breach of copyright is a form of theft – as well being a criminal offence in some jurisdictions, it is potentially a serious breach of professional ethics.

With current technology, things might seem a bit hazy but, basically, without the express permission of BPP Learning Media:

- Photocopying our materials is a breach of copyright

- Scanning, ripcasting or conversion of our digital materials into different file formats, uploading them to facebook or emailing them to your friends is a breach of copyright

You can, of course, sell your books, in the form in which you have bought them – once you have finished with them. (Is this fair to your fellow students? We update for a reason.) Please note the e-products are sold on a single user licence basis: we do not supply 'unlock' codes to people who have bought them secondhand.

And what about outside the UK? BPP Learning Media strives to make our materials available at prices students can afford by local printing arrangements, pricing policies and partnerships which are clearly listed on our website. A tiny minority ignore this and indulge in criminal activity by illegally photocopying our material or supporting organisations that do. If they act illegally and unethically in one area, can you really trust them?

INTRODUCTION

This is BPP Learning Media's AAT Question Bank for External Auditing. It is part of a suite of ground-breaking resources produced by BPP Learning Media for the AAT's assessments under the Qualification and Credit Framework.

The External Auditing assessment will be **computer assessed**. As well as being available in the traditional paper format, this **Question Bank is available in an online environment** containing tasks similar to those you will encounter in the AAT's testing environment. BPP Learning Media believe that the best way to practise for an online assessment is in an online environment. However, if you are unable to practise in the online environment you will find that all tasks in the paper Question Bank have been written in a style that is as close as possible to the style that you will be presented with in your online assessment.

This Question Bank has been written in conjunction with the BPP Text, and has been carefully designed to enable students to practise all of the learning outcomes and assessment criteria for the units that make up External Auditing. It is fully up to date as at June 2013 and reflects both the AAT's unit guide and the sample assessment(s) provided by the AAT.

This Question Bank contains these key features:

- tasks corresponding to each chapter of the Text. Some tasks are designed for learning purposes, others are of assessment standard

- the AAT's sample assessment(s) and answers for External Auditing and further BPP practice assessments

The emphasis in all tasks and assessments is on the practical application of the skills acquired.

VAT

You may find tasks throughout this Question Bank that need you to calculate or be aware of a rate of VAT. This is stated at 20% in these examples and questions.

Approaching the assessment

When you sit the assessment it is very important that you follow the on screen instructions. This means you need to carefully read the instructions, both on the introduction screens and during specific tasks.

When you access the assessment you should be presented with an introductory screen with information similar to that shown below (taken from the introductory screen from the AAT's AQ2013 Sample Assessments for External Auditing).

> We have provided the following assessment to help you familiarise yourself with AAT's e-assessment environment. It is designed to demonstrate as many as possible of the question types you may find in a live assessment. It is not designed to be used on its own to determine whether you are ready for a live assessment.
>
> Please note that in this practice test only your responses to tasks 1-12, 14-19, 21-22 and 24-32 are marked. Equivalents of tasks 13, 20 and 23 will be human marked in the live assessment.
>
> This assessment contains <u>32 tasks</u> and you should attempt and aim to complete EVERY task.
> Each task is independent. You will not need to refer to your answers to previous tasks.
> Read every task carefully to make sure you understand what is required.
>
> Where the date is relevant, it is given in the task data.
>
> Both minus signs and brackets can be used to indicate negative numbers UNLESS task instructions say otherwise.
>
> You must use a full stop to indicate a decimal point.
> For example, write 100.57 NOT 100,57 or 100 57
>
> You may use a comma to indicate a number in the thousands, but you don't have to.
> For example, 10000 and 10,000 are both OK.
>
> Other indicators are not compatible with the computer-marked system.
>
> Complete all 32 tasks

The actual instructions will vary depending on the subject you are studying for. It is very important you read the instructions on the introductory screen and apply them in the assessment. You don't want to lose marks when you know the correct answer just because you have not entered it in the right format.

In general, the rules set out in the AAT Sample Assessments for the subject you are studying for will apply in the real assessment, but you should again read the information on this screen in the real assessment carefully just to make sure. This screen may also confirm the VAT rate used if applicable.

A full stop is needed to indicate a decimal point. We would recommend using minus signs to indicate negative numbers and leaving out the comma signs to indicate thousands, as this results in a lower number of key strokes and less margin for error when working under time pressure. Having said that, you can use whatever is easiest for you as long as you operate within the rules set out for your particular assessment.

You have to show competence in both sections of assessments and you should therefore complete all of the tasks. Don't leave questions unanswered.

In some assessments written or complex tasks may be human marked. In this case you are given a blank space or table to enter your answer into. You are told in the assessments which tasks these are (note: there may be none if all answers are marked by the computer).

If these involve calculations, it is a good idea to decide in advance how you are going to lay out your answers to such tasks by practising answering them on a word document, and certainly you should try all such tasks in this question bank and in the AAT's environment using the sample/practice assessments.

When asked to fill in tables, or gaps, never leave any blank even if you are unsure of the answer. Fill in your best estimate.

Note that for some assessments where there is a lot of scenario information or tables of data provided (eg tax tables), you may need to access these via 'pop-ups'. Instructions will be provided on how you can bring up the necessary data during the assessment.

Finally, take note of any task specific instructions once you are in the assessment. For example you may be asked to enter a date in a certain format or to enter a number to a certain number of decimal places.

Remember you can practise the BPP questions in this question bank in an online environment on our dedicated AAT Online page. On the same page is a link to the current AAT Sample Assessments as well.

If you have any comments about this book, please e-mail ianblackmore@bpp.com or write to Ian Blackmore, AAT Product Manager, BPP Learning Media Ltd, BPP House, Aldine Place, London W12 8AA.

BPP
LEARNING MEDIA

Question bank

External Auditing Question Bank

Chapter 1 The audit environment

Task 1.1

Which ONE of the following records is a business entity registered as a company not required to keep?

Records of money spent and received by the company from day to day and what the money related to (sales, purchases and wages) ☐

Returns from customers and suppliers ☐

Details of the assets and liabilities of the company ☐

Statements of stock (inventory) held at the financial year end ☐

Task 1.2

Registered companies must have an audit.

Complete the following statement on what an audit is, by filling in the gaps.

An audit is an [▼] by an [▼] [▼] examiner to ensure that the [▼] of a company, prepared from the accounting records by the [▼] give a [▼] of the company's affairs and transactions in the year.

Picklist:

Examination
Directors
Balances
True and fair view
Balance sheet
Auditors
Independent
Assurance
Financial statements
Correct
Qualified

Task 1.3

Select whether the following statements in respect of who is exempt from the requirement to have an audit are true or false.

Private companies with a turnover of less than £6.5 million and a balance sheet total of less than £3.26 million are exempt from the requirement to have an audit.	▼
Public companies with a turnover of less than £6.5 million and a balance sheet total of less than £3.26 million are exempt from the requirement to have an audit.	▼
All companies for whom it has been unnecessary to record a transaction in the financial year are exempt from the requirement to have an audit.	▼

Picklist:

True
False

Task 1.4

Select whether the following statements in respect of the requirement to keep accounting records are true or false.

	True	False
Companies must keep accounting records that are sufficient to disclose with complete accuracy at all times, the financial position of the company.	☐	☐
Companies must keep accounting records that are sufficient to disclose with reasonable accuracy at the company's accounting year end, the financial position of the company.	☐	☐
Companies must keep accounting records that are sufficient to disclose with reasonable accuracy at all times the financial position of the company.	☐	☐

Task 1.5

For the last few years your firm has helped Celina, a sole trader, prepare her accounts for HM Revenue and Customs. Celina is about to incorporate her business and has asked for your advice on the advantages to the company of having its accounts audited (you may assume that the company would be able to claim exemption from audit).

Set out the advantages of an audit for the benefit of Celina.

Task 1.6

Select whether the following statements in respect of the Financial Reporting Council are true or false.

The Financial Reporting Council (FRC) is an independent body that issues professional guidance for auditors to follow.	▼
The Government has delegated responsibility for standard setting and monitoring to the FRC.	▼
Auditors in the UK are required to follow the professional standards issued by the FRC.	▼
These standards are standards on how to audit, known as International Standards on Auditing (UK and Ireland) and Ethical Standards, which outline how auditors should behave and, in particular, how they should remain independent of their clients.	▼

Picklist:

True
False

Task 1.7

Select whether the following statements in respect of the role of the International Audit and Assurance Standards Board (IAASB) are true or false.

IAASB is committed to producing high quality audit standards and promoting international convergence in auditing practice.	▼
IAASB is a constituent body of the Financial Reporting Council (FRC), which is the independent regulator of accounting and auditing in the UK.	▼
When IAASB prepares new standards, it first researches the standard and drafts it, then subjects it to public comment, before issuing it after approval from 51% of the board.	▼

Picklist:

True
False

Task 1.8

You have started work for a company that is in the process of being audited for the first time. The directors have heard that the auditors do not certify that the accounts are correct but instead speak of obtaining reasonable assurance and eventually expressing an opinion on the truth and fairness of the accounts.

Select which concept relates to each statement.

The auditor does not examine each and every transaction in detail to ensure that it is correctly recorded and properly presented.	▼
The view given in accounts is based on a combination of both fact and judgement and therefore cannot be characterised as either 'absolute' or 'correct'.	▼
The financial statements should comply with expected standards and rules, for example, UK GAAP.	▼

Picklist:

Reasonable assurance
Truth
Fairness

Task 1.9

Select which one of the following is not a limitation of auditing by ticking the appropriate box.

The fact that the directors make subjective judgements in preparing the financial statements and there are instances where a range of values could be acceptable ☐

The fact that the directors might not provide the auditors with all the information they need, either intentionally or unintentionally ☐

The fact that fraud may be being concealed, even by falsifying documents which might reasonably appear genuine ☐

The fact that accounting systems are subject to human error ☐

Task 1.10

Select whether the following statements in respect of auditors' working papers are true or false.

Working papers are prepared by the external auditor because there is a professional requirement to do so.	▼
The primary reason for recording work in working papers is so that senior staff members can review junior staff members' work.	▼
Working papers should record contentious issues and how they were resolved.	▼

Picklist:

True
False

Task 1.11

There are two types of assurance engagement which a practitioner is permitted to perform – a reasonable assurance engagement and a limited assurance engagement.

Identify which type of assurance engagement an external audit is by selecting the appropriate option.

An external audit conducted under International Standards on Auditing is

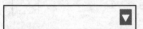

Picklist:

A reasonable assurance engagement
A limited assurance engagement

Chapter 2 The company environment (controls)

Task 2.1

Which ONE of the following is the correct list of the components of an internal control system?

Control environment, risk assessment process, control activities ☐

Control activities, controls monitoring ☐

Control environment, risk assessment process, information systems, internal audit activities, controls monitoring ☐

Control environment, risk assessment process, information system, control activities, controls monitoring ☐

Task 2.2

Select whether the following statements in respect of the control environment are true or false.

The control environment is the attitudes, awareness and actions of management and those charged with governance about internal control and its importance.	▼
If the directors follow control activities themselves and encourage others to do so, if they promote an attitude in a company that internal control is important, and encourage staff to monitor their own performance and the performance of others in observing control, then they can contribute to an excellent control environment.	▼
If directors override controls set up in a company and give other staff the impression that controls are not important, then they will be strongly contributing to a good control environment.	▼

Picklist:

True
False

Task 2.3

An information system is an infrastructure which carries information for a company and compiles a body of information from individual pieces of information. For example, a sales invoice is entered into the information system and is converted into information about overall sales for the month or the year.

Select which is the type of information system described.

An information system that is heavily documented in physical ledgers.	▼
A system which is retained predominantly in electronic format.	▼

Picklist:

Manual
Computerised

Task 2.4

Control activities are the policies and procedures that help ensure that management directives about internal control are carried out. They are often simply referred to as 'controls'.

Select the type of control activity described.

A company will not place an order for goods until a senior member of staff has confirmed that order.	▼
A company locks the storeroom so that raw materials cannot be accessed.	▼
An accounts department is organised so that Debbie is in charge of invoicing and Phil is in charge of receipts.	▼

Picklist:

Performance reviews
Information processing
Physical controls
Segregation of duties

Task 2.5

An external auditor is required to obtain an understanding of the control environment within an audited entity.

Identify whether the following factors contribute to a strong control environment or a weak control environment by selecting the appropriate option.

	Strong	Weak
Directors document control policies and procedures and communicate them to all staff.	☐	☐
Directors demand staff push themselves to obtain goals and promote the concept of 'by any means possible'.	☐	☐
A director has perpetrated a fraud.	☐	☐

Task 2.6

The external auditor may seek to place reliance on internal controls in order to restrict substantive testing.

In each of the following circumstances identify whether the external auditor is likely to place reliance or place no reliance on controls by selecting the appropriate option.

	Reliance	No reliance
A company where there is an internal audit function which monitors controls on a systematic and regular basis.	☐	☐
A small company where the owner-manager has virtual control over all accounting transactions, aided by his part-time, unqualified wife.	☐	☐

Task 2.7

Accounting systems have control objectives and control procedures to mitigate the risks that the control objective is not met.

Identify whether each of the following is a control objective, risk, or control procedure in respect of a sales system by selecting the appropriate option.

Customers do not pay for the goods.	▼
Customers should pay promptly for goods.	▼
Customers are allocated credit limits.	▼

Picklist:

Control objective
Risk
Control procedure

Task 2.8

Accounting systems have control objectives and control procedures to mitigate the risks that the control objective is not met.

Identify whether each of the following is a control objective, risk, or control procedure in respect of a sales system by selecting the appropriate option.

A company intends to invoice all despatches correctly.	▼
A company can match despatch records with invoices prior to invoices being sent out.	▼
A company can send out goods and not invoice them.	▼

Picklist:

Control objective
Risk
Control procedure

Task 2.9

Accounting systems have control objectives and control procedures to mitigate the risks that the control objective is not met.

Identify whether each of the following is a control objective, risk, or control procedure in respect of a purchases system by selecting the appropriate option.

Company pays for goods it has not received.	▼
Company only accepts goods it has ordered.	▼
Company compares invoices to purchase orders and GRNs	▼

Picklist:

Control objective
Risk
Control procedure

Task 2.10

You have begun the audit of Glad Rags Limited, a textiles company. Review the information given about the purchases and payables system given below.

Accounting systems information – Glad Rags Limited

Purchases

The company keeps basic inventories of all the fabric and threads required to manufacture goods from their catalogue. When inventories fall to a certain level, the stores manager requisitions a pre-set amount of that inventory. There are certain fabrics that are only used for a limited number of inventories. That fabric will only be re-ordered if a sales order is placed for items requiring the fabric.

When the purchases department receive a requisition, they place the order with the approved supplier at a prearranged price. An order document is written out and kept in the orders pending file.

When the fabric or thread is received, the stores manager ensures that the quality is suitable and checks the goods against the order. The order is then passed to the accounts department and placed in the pending invoices file.

When the invoice is received, the accounts assistant, Beth Simpkins, checks the invoices against the order to ensure the price and quantity are correct and checks the VAT has been calculated correctly. She initials the invoices to show that these checks have been carried out and gives the invoice a sequence number. The invoice is then entered into the purchase ledger on the computer.

Beth prepares cheques for payment at the end of each two weeks and passes them to the director, Gladys Barton, for signature and approval. The invoices are included with the cheques as evidence of the debt.

Most suppliers send statements at the end of the month which Beth reconciles to the purchase ledger balances. The purchase ledger control account is agreed to the total of the purchase ledger balances at the end of the month.

Identify the control procedures that are present in Glad Rags' system.

Task 2.11

Accounting systems have control objectives and control procedures to mitigate the risks that the control objective is not met.

Identify whether each of the following is a control objective, risk, or control procedure in respect of a purchases system by selecting the appropriate option.

A company wants to pay the right amount for goods purchased.		▼
A company reconciles supplier statements to the purchase ledger.		▼
A company may pay for goods which are used for personal purposes.		▼

Picklist:

Control objective
Risk
Control procedure

Task 2.12

Accounting systems have control objectives and control procedures to mitigate the risks that the control objective is not met.

Identify whether each of the following is a control objective, risk, or control procedure in respect of a wages system by selecting the appropriate option.

The company should pay employees for work done.	▼
The company could make incorrect payments to HMRC.	▼
The company reviews payroll against budgets.	▼

Picklist:

Control objective
Risk
Control procedure

Task 2.13

Accounting systems have control objectives and control procedures to mitigate the risks that the control objective is not met.

Identify whether each of the following is a control objective, risk, or control procedure in respect of a capital expenditure system by selecting the appropriate option.

The company buys assets it does not need.	▼
Depreciation rates should reflect the useful life of an asset.	▼
The company keeps a non current assets register.	▼

Picklist:

Control objective
Risk
Control procedure

Task 2.14

Accounting systems have control objectives and control procedures to mitigate the risks that the control objective is not met.

Identify whether each of the following is a control objective, risk, or control procedure in respect of a purchases system by selecting the appropriate option.

Goods inwards are checked and recorded.	▼
Goods may be used for personal gain.	▼
Goods are available when required for use in the business.	▼

Picklist:

Control objective
Risk
Control procedure

....

Task 2.15

Which ONE of the following is not an inherent limitation of an internal control system?

Employees may make mistakes implementing controls

Controls may have been badly designed by management

Employees and third parties may collude to circumvent controls

Controls may be too expensive to operate on a daily basis

....

Task 2.16

All control systems are subject to limitations, hence the auditor cannot rely solely on controls testing.

Identify the type of limitation described in each statement by selecting the appropriate option.

The payroll clerk and the human resources manager, who authorises the payroll on a monthly basis, are working together to defraud the company by benefiting from the salaries of two false employees.	▼
Sales made to Dixie, a major customer, are always processed at a special discount not recognised by the computer controls, so the sales director always has to process Dixie's sales, and 'fix' the problem.	▼

Picklist:

Collusion
Management override
Human error

....

Task 2.17

An entity uses internal control procedures in order to mitigate the risks to which the entity is exposed. Listed below are two internal control procedures which are applicable to an entity's sales system.

Match each risk mitigated to the internal control procedure by completing the table with the appropriate risk for the procedure.

Internal control procedure	Risk mitigated
Credit checks run on new customers.	
Despatches are checked for quality before leaving the warehouse.	

Picklist:

Customers don't pay promptly

Customers are not good credit risks

Customers are issued credit notes incorrectly

Customers are invoiced incorrectly.

....

Task 2.18

An entity uses internal control procedures in order to mitigate the risks to which the entity is exposed. Listed below are two risks which are applicable to an entity's purchases system.

Match each risk mitigated to the internal control procedure by completing the table with the appropriate procedure for the risk.

Risk	Internal control procedure to mitigate
Company pays for poor quality goods.	
Company pays for the same invoice twice.	

Picklist:

Company reviews all goods inwards for condition.

Company only purchases from approved suppliers.

Company records payments promptly on the purchases ledger.

Company provides supporting evidence of payments before approval.

Chapter 3 Auditing systems

Task 3.1

Which ONE of the following methods are auditors unlikely to use to record company systems?

A Graph
A Flowchart
Narrative notes
A Questionnaire

Task 3.2

Complete the definition below.

A walkthrough test is a test designed to ensure that the system [▼] as the [▼] have been told that it does. They select a transaction in a particular area (for example, a sale or a purchase) and trace it through the company's information system from the initial point (for example, the sales [▼] or the purchase [▼]).

Picklist:

Directors
Staff
Auditors
Operates
Invoice
Goods received note
Order
Supplier statement
Ledger
Requisition

Task 3.3

Use the accounting system information for sales at Glad Rags Limited given below to complete the internal control questionnaire also given below.

Accounting system information

Sales revenue

The company manufactures clothes to order from a catalogue.

When an order is received, the sales department checks that the customer has not exceeded their credit limit and then issues a two-part order document. The sales department fill in the appropriate values for the order. One copy is sent to the production department for the order to be completed and the other is filed alphabetically in the customer file in the sales department.

Once the order is completed, two-part despatch notes are raised. When the factory manager, Ian Jones, has checked the order, one copy of the despatch note is despatched with the goods (to be signed and returned), and one part is matched to the production department's sales order and sent to accounts to raise the invoice. Jane Hill raises the invoices from the order and despatch note, enters them on the computer and sends them out to customers.

Most customers pay in around 60 days. Cheques are passed to Beth Simpkins, one of the accounts assistants, when they come in and she updates the cashbook and the sales ledger. Cheques are banked twice a week. Cheques are kept securely in the safe until banking.

Jane sends out statements to customers each month. Glad Rags' customers are mostly all reputable high street stores and there are rarely irrecoverable debts.

Internal control questionnaire – revenue and receivables system

Question	Yes/No	Comment
Are orders only accepted from low credit risks?		
Are despatches checked by appropriate personnel?		
Are goods sent out recorded?		
Are customers required to give evidence of receipt of goods?		
Are invoices checked to despatch notes and invoices?		
Are invoices prepared using authorised prices?		
Are invoices checked to ensure they add up correctly?		
Are sales receipts matched with invoices?		
Are statements sent out regularly?		
Are overdue accounts reviewed regularly?		
Are there safeguards over post received to ensure that cheques are not intercepted?		
Are bankings made daily?		
Would it be appropriate to perform tests of control in this area? (Give reason/reasons in the comments box.)		

Task 3.4

Teach Co is a company which sends tutors into private homes to assist where children are struggling with their school work. The company provides the tutor, the clients are required to provide materials, which are planned on the first visit. Tutors collect fees per session at the end of each session.

Which ONE of the following combinations of accounting systems are likely to be subject to external audit?

Sales revenue, payroll, cash ☐

Sales revenue, payroll, receivables ☐

Sales revenue, cash, inventory, payables ☐

Sales revenue, cash, receivables and payables ☐

Task 3.5

Once auditors have assessed control risk, they choose an overall approach to the audit.

Identify whether the following statements about audit approach are true or false by selecting the appropriate option.

	True	False
The auditor may take a combined approach, where he will test controls and then reduce his subsequent substantive testing (although he must always carry out tests of detail on material items).	☐	☐
The auditor may take a substantive approach, where he does not test controls, but instead renders control risk as high and conducts more tests of detail instead.	☐	☐

Task 3.6

The external auditor may seek to place reliance on internal controls in order to restrict substantive testing.

For each of the following circumstances, identify the most likely approach to be adopted by the external auditor by selecting the appropriate option.

	Reliance	No reliance
The directors of LightLynx Ltd demand close attention to control procedures, and they monitor how the system is operating on a monthly basis.	☐	☐
At Simlaglow Ltd, there is an accounting staff of two, the financial controller, and his assistant.	☐	☐
There are ten people in the accounts department at Luxicon Ltd. The financial controller keeps a close interest in all transactions, and often intervenes to speed up proceedings.	☐	☐

Task 3.7

Two types of computer-assisted audit techniques (CAAT) are test data and audit software.

For each of the procedures listed below, select the type of CAAT which would be used to perform that procedure.

Selection of a sample of sales ledger accounts over £30,000.	▼
Input of sales invoices with false customer numbers to ensure application controls function correctly.	▼
Analytical procedures on statement of comprehensive income, on a line by line approach.	▼

Picklist:

Audit software
Test data

Task 3.8

An external auditor is required to obtain an understanding of the control environment within an audited entity.

Identify whether the following factors contribute to a strong control environment or a weak control environment by selecting the appropriate option.

Management communicate controls values to staff and ensure new staff are thoroughly training in controls procedures.	▼
Management emphasise the importance of targets over procedures.	▼
Management include adherence to company procedures in annual appraisals for staff members.	▼

Picklist:

Strong
Weak

Task 3.9

The following are descriptions of procedures within the sales system of a company.

Identify whether each procedure indicates a strength or a weakness in the system by selecting the appropriate option.

	Strength	Weakness
Julie raises the sales invoices on the basis of the goods received notes she is sent by the warehouse. She inputs the information, prints the invoices, and sends them out. No other procedures are carried out.	☐	☐
Statements are sent to customers on a monthly basis.	☐	☐

Task 3.10

During the audit of Daffodilly Limited, it was discovered that although the company had good controls over sales ordering and invoicing, controls over cash receipts were weak. The following weakness was noted:

Weakness: receipts

Post opening appears to be unsupervised and no initial list of receipts is made. Customer remittances do not appear to be retained.

Prepare extracts, suitable for inclusion in a report to management of Daffodilly Limited, which set out:

(i)   **The possible consequences of this weakness, and**
(ii) **Recommendations you would make**

Task 3.11

The following is a list of controls in the system at Daredevil Ltd.

Identify how an auditor would test these controls by matching the control with the relevant test. If necessary, you can use the same answer twice. Some controls may require two tests.

Controls	Tests of control
The company has a policy for choosing suppliers	
Goods received are examined for quantity and quality	
Goods received are checked against the order	

Picklist:

Review a sample of orders
Observe the stores manager receiving some goods
Observe the accounts assistant checking supplier invoices
Scrutinise paid invoices
Scrutinise reconciliations

Task 3.12

The following is a list of controls in the system at Daredevil Ltd.

Identify how an auditor would best test these controls, by matching each control with the tests below. (Some answers may be used more than once.)

Controls	Tests of control
Hours worked are recorded	
Hours worked are reviewed	
Payroll is prepared by a director	

Picklist:

Review clockcards
Review payroll
Observe director
Observe staff arriving at work

Task 3.13

During the audit of Zhong Limited, the following weaknesses in general computer controls were discovered:

- No passwords are required to access any part of the computerised accounting system
- While security backup copies of files are taken, these copies are kept in the desk occupied by the accounts clerk.

Prepare extracts, suitable for inclusion in a report to management of Zhong Limited, which set out:

(i) **The possible consequences of these weaknesses, and**
(ii) **Recommendations you would make in respect of them**

Task 3.14

The following are descriptions of procedures within the purchases system of Kingsley Ltd.

For each procedure, state whether it indicates a strength or a weakness in the system.

Sandra reconciles supplier statements with the purchase ledger as she receives them.	▼
Payments, which are approved by a director, are made on a monthly basis on the basis of a printout of due items from the purchase ledger.	▼

Picklist:

Strength
Weakness

Task 3.15

The following are descriptions of procedures within the payroll system of Weasley Ltd.

Identify whether each procedure indicates a strength or a weakness in the system by selecting the appropriate option.

Each member of staff is allocated a personnel file on arrival, which is updated for any changes in pay rates or hours.	▼
The payroll is created by the wages clerk on the last Thursday of a month. She runs the payroll package which automatically produces a bank payments list and notifies the bank to pay the salaries.	▼

Picklist:

Strength
Weakness

Task 3.16

The following are descriptions of procedures within the non current assets system of Primrose Ltd.

For each procedure, identify whether it indicates a strength or a weakness in the system by selecting the appropriate option.

	Strength	Weakness
The company maintains a non current asset register. The operations manager checks the register to physical assets once a year.	☐	☐
The operations manager and the purchasing director meet monthly to discuss asset requirements for the business.	☐	☐

Task 3.17

The following are descriptions of procedures within the inventory system of Calend Ltd.

For each procedure, identify whether it indicates a strength or a weakness in the system by selecting the appropriate option.

Inventory is kept in a locked store, secured by the key card system in operation at the company. All members of staff are issued with key cards.	▼
The production manager reviews levels of inventory and makes requisitions on a monthly basis.	▼

Picklist:

Strength
Weakness

Task 3.18

During the audit of Miraglow Ltd, it was discovered that although the company maintained a central list of suppliers, the purchase team did not necessarily use it and often used different suppliers offering better prices.

Prepare extracts, suitable for inclusion in a report to management of Miraglow Ltd, which set out:

(i) **The possible consequences, and**
(ii) **The recommendations that you would make in respect of this matter.**

Task 3.19

ISA 265 *Communicating deficiencies in internal control to those charged with governance and management* defines a significant deficiency in internal control as a deficiency or combination of deficiencies in internal control that, in the auditors professional judgement, is of sufficient importance to merit the attention of those charged with governance.

Identify whether or not the following deficiency in internal control is a significant deficiency by selecting the appropriate option:

The identification of a fraud, relating to a material monetary amount, carried out by a director of the audited entity, which was not prevented by the entity's internal control system.

▼

Picklist:

Not a significant deficiency
Significant deficiency

Chapter 4 Assessing risks

Task 4.1

Identify whether the following statements in respect of obtaining an understanding of the business are true or false by selecting the appropriate option.

Auditors are required to obtain an understanding of the entity and its environment only when the client is a new client.	▼
Auditors are required to obtain an understanding of the entity and its environment so that they are able to assess the risks relating to the audit.	▼

Picklist:

True
False

Task 4.2

Complete the following statements about audit risk.

Audit risk is the risk that the auditors give an inappropriate opinion on the financial statements. It is made up of three components:

- [▼] risk – risks arising as a result of the nature of the business, its transactions and environment

- [▼] risk – the risk that the control system at the company does not detect, correct or prevent misstatements

  (These two risks combined are the risk that misstatements will exist in the financial statements in the first place)

- [▼] risk – the risk that auditors do not discover misstatements in the financial statements

Picklist:

Auditing
Human
Inherent
Accounts
Detection
Business
Control

Task 4.3

The auditor takes a number of steps after gaining an understanding of a client and its environment.

Which ONE of the following steps would NOT be taken?

(1) Identify inherent and control risks while obtaining an understanding of the entity ☐

(2) Relate identified risks to what could go wrong at a financial statement level ☐

(3) Consider if the risks could cause material misstatement ☐

(4) Identify detection risk as part of a review of audit firm procedure ☐

Task 4.4

Set out what can go wrong with balances, transactions and events at a financial statement level.

Task 4.5

Identify whether the following statements about materiality are true or false by selecting the appropriate option.

	True	False
Materiality is the concept of importance to users.	☐	☐
It is relevant to auditors because they will only test items which are material.	☐	☐
Calculating materiality and selecting samples on the basis of materiality helps the auditor to reduce audit risk to an acceptable level.	☐	☐

Task 4.6

Which ONE of the following does not suggest a significant risk?

A risk of fraud ☐

A complex transaction ☐

A significant transaction with a related party ☐

A transaction in the normal course of business for the entity ☐

....

Task 4.7

Using the background information given below, identify two areas of risk for the audit of Glad Rags Limited, explaining why they are risks. You should also set out what could go wrong at a financial statement level in respect of each risk.

Background information

Glad Rags Limited is a private company set up by Bill and Gladys Burton 50 years ago. It manufactures clothes which it sells mainly to high street clothing stores. The company relies heavily on two major customers: British Clothes Stores (BCS) and Value Mart (VM). The company has another 20 customers on the sales ledger, but BCS and VM account for 60% of revenue. BCS have recently told Gladys that they are auditing their suppliers to ensure that the suppliers meet their stringent quality requirements. Glad Rags has three major suppliers (Fine Fabrics, The Fabric Wholesaler and Terry's Threads).

The company is 100% owned by Gladys Burton, who inherited her husband's shares when he died in 20X0. She is the sole director. Gladys has no children to inherit the business and has confided to the auditors that she is thinking of selling the business in the near future. Her plans are not known to any other members of staff at Glad Rags.

Your audit firm has been the auditor for 5 years. The firm has always found Gladys to be honest and reliable. Gladys has a key role in the day to day running of the business. She oversees the production of the company sales catalogue, runs the personnel department (hiring and firing staff and dealing with the payroll) and determines which suppliers the company will use.

Revenue is £7 million with gross profit at 30% and profit for the year of 9.5%.

Gladys employs a part-time bookkeeper (Bill Overton) to oversee the two accounts assistants (Jane and Beth) and to produce monthly and annual accounts. Including these staff members and Gladys, there are 8 administrative staff and 50 machinists/cutters.

Materiality has been set at £70,000 for this year's audit.

Task 4.8

Listed below are two risks that the auditors have noted at Linklynx Ltd.

Identify what could go wrong at a financial statement level in each situation by selecting the appropriate option.

The company issues inventory to customers on a sale or return basis.	▼
The non current asset register is not reconciled regularly with the actual assets.	▼

Picklist:

Assets could be overstated
Assets could be understated
Assets could be over- or understated

Task 4.9

When planning an audit of financial statements, the external auditor is required to consider how factors such as the entity's operating environment and its system of internal control affect the risk of misstatement in the financial statements.

Identify whether the following factors are likely to increase or reduce the risk of misstatement.

	Increase	Reduce
The company operates in a highly regulated industry.	☐	☐
The company has an internal audit function committed to monitoring internal controls.	☐	☐
The company has set ambitious growth targets for all its salesmen, to be judged at the end of the financial year.	☐	☐

Task 4.10

The external auditor assesses control risk in order to determine the audit approach.

Identify whether the following factors are likely to lead to the auditor assessing that there is an increase or decrease in control risk.

	Increase	Decrease
The role of sales ledger clerk has been filled by four different people during the year, following the retirement of a long-standing sales ledger clerk at the end of last year.	☐	☐
The financial controller is a qualified accountant, as are two of his high level staff.	☐	☐
The directors have a positive attitude towards controls and enforce them company-wide.	☐	☐

Task 4.11

Complete the following sentences.

A control such as a [▼] may [▼] unauthorised access to a computer programme so that errors cannot be deliberately input.

Alternatively a control such as a reconciliation [▼] mistakes, which the person carrying out the reconciliation can then [▼] , so that there is no misstatement in the financial statements as a result.

Picklist:

Reconciliation
Password
Detects
Prevent
Correct
Reject

Task 4.12

Complete the definition.

Material and pervasive is taken to mean that the misstatement is:

- [▼] to one item in the financial statements

- [▼] to one item, but the item could represent a substantial portion of the financial statements

- If relating to a disclosure, [▼] to users' understanding of the financial statements.

Picklist:

Confined
Not confined
Important
Fundamental
Judgemental

Chapter 5 Audit planning

Task 5.1

Identify whether the following statements in respect of the audit strategy and the audit plan are true or false by selecting the appropriate option.

The audit strategy is the overall approach for carrying out the audit.		▼
The audit plan contains detailed instructions for testing each audit area.		▼

Picklist:

True
False

Task 5.2

Which ONE of the following will the audit team NOT discuss at a planning meeting?

The responsibilities of each audit team member with regard to the audit and their duty of professional scepticism ☐

Whether the audit should be accepted by the firm ☐

Any issues, including confidential issues, the audit team should be aware of prior to the audit ☐

The susceptibility of the financial statements to misstatements and audit risks ☐

Task 5.3

Identify whether the following statements concerning evidence are true or false by selecting the appropriate option

An auditor needs to obtain sufficient, appropriate evidence.		▼
Sufficient means evidence from at least two sources.		▼

Picklist:

True
False

Task 5.4

Auditors use tests of controls and substantive procedures to gather audit evidence.

For each of the procedures below, identify whether it is a test of control or a substantive procedure.

	Test of control	Substantive procedure
Observation of inventory count	☐	☐
Inspection of an invoice to vouch cost of new non current asset	☐	☐
Recalculation of depreciation charge	☐	☐

Task 5.5

You are planning the audit of Glad Rags Limited. Materiality has been set at £70,000.

Using the extracts from the statement of financial position below, select which of the items listed below is likely to be subject to mainly analytical procedures or tests of detail.

STATEMENT OF FINANCIAL POSITION FOR GLAD RAGS LIMITED
Year ended 30 November 20X4

	20X4		20X3	
	£	£	£	£
Non current assets		21,940		24,794
Current assets				
Inventory	352,599		302,214	
Receivables	1,345,933		1,412,911	
Bank	29,583	1,728,115	23,491	1,738,616
Net current assets		1,750,055		1,763,410
Payables: amounts falling due				
within one year		(365,038)		(355,893)
		1,385,017		1,407,517

Non current assets	▼
Inventory	▼
Receivables	▼
Bank	▼
Payables	▼

Picklist:

Analytical procedures
Tests of details

Task 5.6

The accountant at Forsythe Limited has presented you with a draft statement of financial position for the year, which is given below. The audit manager has suggested that it is likely that materiality will be set at £65,000.

Select which balances below should be tested in detail and which should be reviewed using analytical procedures.

Draft statement of financial position for Forsythe Limited year ended 31 December 20X4

	20X4 £	20X4 £	20X3 £	20X3 £
Non current assets		3,812,594		3,862,591
Current assets				
Inventory	423,781		405,863	
Receivables	10,020		9,930	
Bank balance	–		25,795	
		433,801		441,588
Current liabilities				
Bank overdraft	(17,000)			
Trade payables	(226,313)		(220,879)	
Accruals	(32,476)		(29,583)	
Bank loan	(100,000)		(100,000)	
		(375,789)		(350,462)
Long term liabilities				
Bank loan		(2,425,000)		(2,525,000)
		1,445,606		1,428,717

Non current assets	▼
Inventory	▼
Receivables	▼
Bank	▼
Trade payables	▼
Accruals	▼
Bank loan	▼

Picklist:

Analytical procedures
Tests of details

Task 5.7

Complete the table below. In the left-hand column you should list the financial statement assertions and in the right-hand column give an example of a test that fulfils each assertion.

Financial statement assertion	Example test

Task 5.8

When selecting items in order to perform tests of controls, the auditor has to consider a number of factors.

For each of the following factors, identify whether they will result in an increase or decrease in sample size by selecting the appropriate option.

Auditor intends to increase his reliance on tests of controls.	▼
Auditor is selecting a sample of sales invoices, when a new customer means the volume of sales at the client has increased by 20%.	▼
Auditors' tolerable deviation rate rises from 1.5% to 2%.	▼

Picklist:

Increase
Decrease
No effect

Task 5.9

The objective of a substantive test will determine the population from which the sample for testing is selected.

For each of the objectives set out below, match the population from which the sample should be selected.

Obtain evidence of the completeness of the trade payables balance.	
Obtain evidence that the bank balance is fairly stated.	

Picklist:

Bank statement
Purchase ledger
Purchase requisition
Purchase invoice
Bank reconciliation
Bank letter
Cash book

Task 5.10

The external auditor is required to undertake analytical procedures as part of the planning process in order to identify the risk of misstatement of figures in the financial statements. The results of some analytical procedures carried out on sales are listed below.

Identify the most likely conclusion to be drawn as a result of the procedures undertaken.

Sales revenue has increased by 3% but the gross profit margin is down by 1.5%		▼
Sales in the last month of the year were 5% higher than in previous years, and also 4% higher than the average for a month for the company.		▼

Picklist:

Sales revenue may be overstated
Sales revenue may be understated
More information required to draw a conclusion

Task 5.11

Identify whether the following statements concerning selecting items for testing are true or false by selecting the appropriate option.

When sampling, the auditor must ensure that all sampling items have an equal chance of selection.	▼
When an auditor selects a sample of invoices at random from the filed invoices for the year, this is known as the random approach to sampling.	▼

Picklist:

True
False

Task 5.12

As part of verification techniques in respect of repairs and maintenance expense, the auditor inspects invoices. The auditor will gain assurance about different assertions depending on the information on the invoice.

In respect of the information below, identify the assertion for which that information will provide assurance by selecting the appropriate option.

Description on the invoice.	▼
Date on the invoice.	▼

Picklist:

Classification
Cut off
Accuracy

Task 5.13

Auditors use tests of controls and substantive procedures to gather audit evidence.

For each of the procedures below, identify whether it is a test of control or substantive procedure.

	Test of control	Substantive procedure
A test to verify the operation of procedures designed to safeguard the business.	☐	☐
A comparison of financial and non-financial information by the auditor.	☐	☐
A test to verify an assertion made in the financial statements.	☐	☐

BPP
LEARNING MEDIA

Chapter 6 Audit of inventory

Task 6.1

Which ONE of the following company controls is a key factor in auditing whether the inventories in the financial statements actually exist?

The inventory count ☐

Inventory records ☐

The locked stores ☐

The reorder levels ☐

Task 6.2

Match the following situations with their effect on the financial statements by completing the table.

The company records a sale but the inventory is also counted as existing at the year end.	(i) (ii)
The company accept goods on the day of the inventory count, which get included in the count, but do not record the invoice in purchases until the following year.	(i) (ii)

Picklist:

Profit is overstated
Profit is understated
Assets are overstated
Assets are understated
Liabilities are overstated
Liabilities are understated

Task 6.3

When auditing the value of finished goods, set out what components of cost auditors will need to verify, and what evidence they will seek in respect of those components.

```
┌─────────────────────────────────────────────────────────────────────┐
│                                                                       │
│                                                                       │
│                                                                       │
│                                                                       │
│                                                                       │
│                                                                       │
│                                                                       │
│                                                                       │
└─────────────────────────────────────────────────────────────────────┘
```

Task 6.4

Which ONE of the following tests does not contribute to the auditors' assurance that net realisable value of inventory is higher than cost?

Ensuring inventory which appeared damaged at the inventory count has been valued accordingly ☐

Examine sales prices after the year end to ensure that none have significantly dropped (perhaps to below cost) ☐

Review quantities of inventory sold after the year end to ensure that goods are not obsolete ☐

Review sales prices during the year to ensure that none have been significantly low ☐

Task 6.5

You are going to attend the annual inventory count at Glad Rags Limited. Last year's working papers show that the major items in inventories were standard white thread (code: S01) and cotton jersey fabric in black and blue (codes: CJ02 and CJ03). The sample size for test counts was 12.

MEMO

From: Joe Worple, Stores Manager, Glad Rags Limited

To: Audit senior

I enclose the instructions for this year's inventory count, which will take place at 3pm on 30 November. The machines will not be operating during the count. Ten machinists have volunteered to be counters, the rest have accepted a half-day.

There are no new issues relating to inventory this year, except that the company has just bought a large consignment of specialist fabric A001 to service a large order for Value Mart. The reorder levels for most of the standard fabrics have not changed from last year. In December, we shall be starting some major orders for clients for the spring season, so we have a high level of inventory as usual. As you know, our fabric and threads are measured in metres and the bales are marked up with lengths removed. We do not remeasure every bale of fabric.

Most of the fabric and threads are in the stores. The machinists will be asked to finish work in progress at the end of the day before the count. There will be some goods awaiting delivery which are kept in the machining room. We are not planning to make any deliveries on the day of the count and have requested that our suppliers do not make deliveries on the day.

GLAD RAGS LIMITED
INVENTORY COUNT INSTRUCTIONS 30 November 20X4
Overseer – Joe Worple, Stores Manager

Checkers – Betty Fradin, Liz Tyler, Mandeep Singh, Bet King, Elspeth Worthing, Jill Manson, Jane Smith, Bev Jones, Claire King, Ann Jones

All pieces should be finished before the count commences. Machinists should not commence new pieces after 2pm. All finished goods need to be placed in the east end of the machine room to be counted.

Checkers should work in pairs and will be allocated to different areas of the stores. Two checkers will count finished goods in the machine room. Each checker will be issued with a sheet stating the fabrics and threads in their section which they must count. One checker should check the amounts of each fabric and write them down on the sheet. Once a bale has been counted, it must be marked with a red sticker to show that it has been counted. The second checker should check the first checker's work. When an item has been checked for a second time, it should be marked with a green sticker. Joe Worple will carry out random checks on completed inventory sheets to ensure that items have been checked correctly.

Each checking pair should remeasure four bales of fabric to ensure that the record attached to the bale is correct.

No checker must leave until permitted by Joe Worple. Checkers will be paid £6 an hour for the count, which must be noted and authorised by Joe Worple.

Using the information given:

(i) **Set out the key issues at the inventory count.**

(ii) **Appraise the count instructions provided by the company and conclude whether you believe the count will be capable of producing a reliable figure for the existence of inventory.**

Task 6.6

Here is a working paper showing the test carried out on inventory cut off. Materiality is £70,000.

Client:	Glad Rags Ltd		Prepared by:	J Devoran
Accounting date:	30 November 20X4		Date:	2 January 20X5
			Reviewed by:	
			Date:	

Inventory cut off

Last deliveries out

Sales order/GDN	Customer	Agreed to November Sales Day Book
200894/DN12403	Value Mart	✓
200895/DN12404	BCS	✓
200896/DN12405	Tisco Stores	✓

The above items have all been excluded from the inventory count

Last deliveries in (from invoices pending file – these were the only three orders received pending invoices)

Order	Supplier	Agreed to November Purchase Day Book
P1013	Fine Fabrics Ltd	✓
P1017	Fine Fabrics Ltd	✓
P1021	Terry's Threads	*

* This invoice was not received until 15 December and was included in December's Purchase Day Book. The value was £2,476.

All the above items were included in the inventory count.

Identify the appropriate conclusion to draw about inventory cut off at this stage by selecting the appropriate option.	▼

Picklist:

Cut off is fairly stated
Further work is required before a conclusion can be drawn

Task 6.7

Below are the results of the testing carried out at the inventory count of Glad Rags Limited.

Client:	Glad Rags Ltd	Prepared by:	J Devoran
Accounting date:	30 November 20X4	Date:	30 November 20X4
		Reviewed by:	
		Date:	

Inventory existence

Items remeasured

Inventory code	Amount per record	Amount measured	Correct
C01	20.75m	20.75m	Yes
L02	13.45m	13.45m	Yes
S03	2.5m	2.5m	Yes
CJ04	16.75m	16.75m	Yes
CJ05	2.35m	2.35m	Yes

Arithmetical accuracy of records

Inventory code	Record adds?
L01	Yes
L03	Yes
S05	Yes

Conclusion – controls over inventory measurement operate effectively

Test counts

Inventory code	Amount per inventory sheet	Amount physically present	Count correct?
A001	200m	200m	Yes
S01	4 × 50m	4 × 50m	Yes
	1 × 21m	1 × 21m	
CJ02	2 × 50m	2 × 50m	Yes
	1 × 1.35m	1 × 1.35m	
CJ03	2 × 50m	2 × 50m	Yes
	1 × 25.50m	1 × 25.50m	
CJ04	16.75m	16.75m	Yes
S02	4 × 50m	4 × 50m	Yes
	1 × .25m	1 × .25m	
L04	12m	12m	Yes
N01	135m	135m	Yes
N02	127m	127m	Yes
X101 White t-shirts	250	250	Yes
X103 Blue t-shirts	175	175	Yes
Z111 Babygros	1,000	1,000	Yes

Conclusion – test counts indicate count operated efficiently

Identify which of the tests needs to be carried out to draw a conclusion as to whether the existence of inventory is fairly stated by selecting the appropriate option.	▼

Picklist:

Trace test count items to final inventory sheets
Trace test count items to purchase invoices

··

Task 6.8

Grols Ltd designs, prints and configures paper and cardboard packaging to order for customers. It has a large inventory of raw material, work in progress and finished goods. Batches of raw material are indistinguishable, and they are kept on large shelves, and reordered when a reorder limit is reached. The company has experienced the following two problems:

(1) A hole in the factory roof which resulted in a leak in the raw material stores.

(2) The financial difficulties of a major customer, to whom the most recent consignment has not been shipped.

Set out, in a manner suitable for inclusion in the audit plan:

(i) **The audit risks relating to inventory**

(ii) **The procedures to be undertaken in order to ensure that inventory valuation is fairly stated in the financial statements**

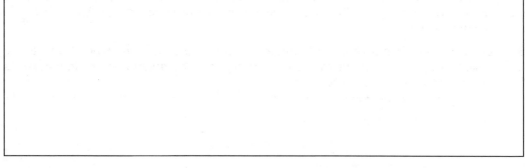

··

Task 6.9

Below are the last goods recorded in and out of the factory on the last day of the financial year (31 December). The invoices in respect of these have been traced to the ledgers.

Last goods in		Traced to
X13639443		December purchase ledger
R0204863		January purchase ledger
Last goods out		
FG135933 – Careys		December sales ledger
FG135934 – Seepe		January sales ledger

Which ONE of the following options shows the item(s) on which cut off is correct?

X13639443 only

FG135933 and X1369443 only

R0204863 and FG135934 only

FG135934 only

Task 6.10

Masterful Ltd operates a perpetual inventory system. The year end is 31 December. Inventory is counted four times a year, in February, May, August and October. The company has a sophisticated computerised system which can identify the value of inventory on hand at any time. The system produces goods in and out notes when inventory comes in or out of the factory, those notes are matched with invoices in the accounts department.

Set out, in a manner suitable for inclusion in the audit plan the procedures to be undertaken in order to ensure that the existence and completeness of inventory is fairly stated in the financial statements.

Chapter 7 Audit of other assets (and related items)

Task 7.1

Which ONE of the following audit tests is NOT a test of completeness of non current assets?

Obtain a summary of non current assets and reconcile with the opening position (additions and disposals) ☐

Compare non current assets in the general ledger with the non current asset register and obtain explanations for any differences ☐

Inspect assets to see if they are in use and good condition ☐

Check that assets which physically exist are included in the register ☐

Task 7.2

Identify the assertion at which each of the following audit tests are directed by selecting the appropriate option.

Review depreciation rates for reasonableness (given asset lives, residual values, replacement policy, possible obsolescence)	▼
Vouch title deeds of buildings.	▼
Inspect a sample of assets listed in the non current assets register.	▼

Picklist:

Rights and obligations
Existence
Valuation

Task 7.3

It is 10 November 20X3 and you have been asked to work on the audit of the non current asset section of the accounts of Kandistors Limited for the year ended 31 December 20X3. The company manufactures sweets and chocolate which it sells and delivers to the retail trade.

The partner in charge of the audit has asked you to examine the non current assets section of the company's most recent management accounts. The company maintains a non current assets register and you should assume that there will be no non current asset acquisitions between the dates of 1 November 20X3 and 31 December 20X3.

Set out, in a manner suitable for inclusion in an audit plan, TEN audit procedures to be carried out to meet the following assertions:

Completeness

Existence

Ownership

Valuation

You are not required to consider disposals of non current assets or depreciation charges.

For each procedure mentioned in your plan, where appropriate, you should identify the associated assertion.

Task 7.4

Which of the following balances must an auditor NOT neglect when selecting a sample for auditing receivables?

(i)   Material balances
(ii)   Old unpaid accounts
(iii) Credit balances
(iv) Zero balances
(v)   Accounts which have been paid by the date of examination

(i) only   ☐

(i) and (ii) only   ☐

(i), (ii), (iii) and (iv) only   ☐

All of them   ☐

Task 7.5

Identify whether the following statements in respect of auditing sales revenue are true or false.

	True	False
Auditors often perform analytical procedures when auditing sales revenue as there is usually a great deal of analytical information about sales revenue (for example, analyses of sales per month or per product) at a company, and sales revenue has a number of predictable relationships (with receivables, with gross margin) so it is a good balance to test by analytical procedures.	☐	☐
Auditors may test understatement of sales revenue by tracing a sale from the general ledger back through the system to the sales order.	☐	☐

Task 7.6

In relation to bank letters, complete the statements below.

Bank letter requests should be made by the ...	▼
Bank letter requests should be sent to the bank ...	▼

Picklist: (for Bank letter requests should be made by the ...)
Directors
Auditors

Picklist: (for Bank letter requests should be sent to the bank ...)
At the year end
A month before the year end
A month after the year end

- -

Task 7.7

Complete the following definition, relevant to the audit of bank.

[▼] is the practice of manipulating when cash receipts and payments are recorded and sent out to manipulate the [▼] results at the year end.

For example, if a company wanted liabilities to look [▼] then it might record a number of payments (which would also therefore be included on the bank reconciliation, reducing the bank balance) but not physically send those cheques out until after the year end, so that in practice, the bank balance is [▼] than it appears to be in the accounts, as is the [▼] balance.

Picklist:
Window dressing
Door closing
Statement of financial position
Statement of comprehensive income
Higher
Lower
Receivables
Payables

- -

Task 7.8

You are continuing your work at Glad Rags Limited. The following is a working paper, showing work done on the receivables balance.

Client:	Glad Rags Ltd		Prepared by:	A Student
Accounting date:	30 November 20X4		Date:	19 January 20X5
			Reviewed by:	
			Date:	

Receivables circularisation

Objective: To ensure that receivables exist and are genuine obligations to the company
Work done: Replies reconciled to sales ledger balances. Where replies not available, cash received after date gives sufficient evidence concerning existence and rights.

Debtor	Balance per sales ledger	Agreed to debtor reply	Comments/reconciliation	Balance Agreed?
	£			
BCS	484,536	No	Difference is a receipt for £44,938	o/s
Brodies	74,973	Yes	–	Yes
Tisco Stores	78,805	No	Difference is requested credit for damaged goods returned.	o/s
Value Mart	323,024	Yes	–	Yes
Cavanaghs	14,388	Yes	–	Yes
H and T	18,933	N/A	Balance agreed to cash receipts in Dec and Jan total £18,933	Yes
Nice Clothes	17,231	N/A	Balance agreed to cash receipts in Dec and Jan total £17,231	Yes
Value Clothes	22,315	Yes	–	Yes

Identify which of Glad Rags Limited's accounting records each of the reconciling items should be checked to, by matching the record with each reconciling item.

(i) **BCS difference** ....

(ii) **Tisco stores difference** ....

Picklist:

Bank statements
Post year end sales ledger
Pre year end sales ledger
Goods received note
Goods returned note

Task 7.9

An audit junior will carry out the audit work on valuation of debts of Glad Rags. An aged trade receivables analysis from the sales ledger at 30 November 20X4 will be available. Glad Rags' standard credit terms are 60 days.

Set out, in a manner suitable for inclusion in an audit plan, the procedures to be performed on receivables valuation.

Task 7.10

Below is a schedule of non current assets at Craftys Limited. The opening figures have already been verified to the prior year audit file and financial statements.

	Land £	Buildings £	Vehicles £	Fittings £	Total £
Cost at 1 January 20X4	1,500,000	2,750,000	128,970	121,173	4,500,143
Additions	–	–	42,000	697	42,697
Cost at 31 December 20X4	1,500,000	2,750,000	170,970	121,870	4,542,840
Accumulated depreciation at 1 January 20X4	–	503,000	66,893	67,659	637,552
Depreciation	–	55,000	25,646	12,048	92,694
Accumulated depreciation at 31 December 20X4	–	558,000	92,539	79,707	730,246
Carrying amount at 1 January 20X4	1,500,000	2,247,000	62,077	53,514	3,862,591
Carrying amount at 31 December 20X4	1,500,000	2,192,000	78,431	42,163	3,812,594

Depreciation rates:

Buildings – 2%
Vehicles – 15%
Fittings – 10%

Set out, in a matter suitable for inclusion in an audit plan, the procedures that should be done to verify that the non current assets figure in the financial statements is true and fair.

Task 7.11

Green Valley Limited is a company owning three garden centres, one of which has a cafe. You have the following information about Green Valley's sales from the prior year audit file:

Sales income	Shop 1	Shop 2	Shop 3	Café
April – July	Average 400 customers per day @ £30			
Feb/March Aug/Sept	Average 300 customers per day @ £20	Average 75% of income of shop 1	Average 65% of income of shop 1	Average ½ customers of shop 1 per day @ £8
Oct – Jan	Average 200 customers per day @ £15			

Perform analytical procedures on this information and select whether the sales income figures below might be under or overstated or appear reasonable.

Shop 1 sales income is £2,521,634	▼
Cafe sales income is £431,996	▼
Total sales income £5,673,676	▼

Picklist:

Understated
Overstated
Appear reasonable

Task 7.12

This is the bank reconciliation at 31 December 20X4 for a company you are auditing. The audit junior has verified the relevant figures to the cashbook and the bank letter as shown.

BANK RECONCILIATION 31 December 20X4			£
Balance per cashbook		CB	(17,000)
Less: 31 Dec takings			(1,278)
Add: Cheque payments	003465		5,398
	003466		2,476
	003467		15,398
	003468		108
	003469		2,365
	003470		3,465
	003471		791
	003472		23
Balance per bank statement		B	11,746
Key: B – agreed to bank letter CB – agreed to cashbook			

Which source of audit evidence must the remaining figures be verified against?

Pre year end cash book ☐

Post year end cash book ☐

Pre year end bank statements ☐

Post year end bank statements ☐

Task 7.13

During the last quarter of year ended 31 December 20X9, Carl Ltd starting supplying a new customer, Diversity Ltd. Carl Ltd had carried out initial credit checks before accepting orders from this customer then began to supply Diversity Ltd goods on standard credit terms of 60 days. The audit is being planned during the last week in December, at which time, Diversity Ltd has not paid any of its balance. Carl Ltd has requested that the auditors do not seek to confirm the balance directly with Diversity, as it is a new customer, and the credit controller does not want to appear to be being heavy handed at the outset of the relationship. The balance at 31 December is material.

Diversity is a relatively new company which has grown exponentially in its field in the first year of business, raising questions in the financial press about its ability to maintain functioning working capital.

Set out, in a manner suitable for inclusion in the audit plan:

(i) The audit risks relating to this receivable balance

(ii) The procedures to be undertaken to ensure that it is fairly stated in the financial statements

Task 7.14

As part of your work on non-current assets, you have reviewed the repairs and maintenance expense code. You have found the following material items there.

Repair to main jigsaw	£24,000
Replacement engine	£25,000
Maintenance contract with Micheals	£12,000
New computer software for sales	£8,000

By how much should additions to non-current assets be increased?

£69,000	☐
£57,000	☐
£33,000	☐
£25,000	☐

Task 7.15

During the external audit of Bream Ltd, the audit junior identified two instances of the sales ledger clerk allocating later receipts against earlier invoices. The instances related to the same account, and she discovered them when focusing on the receipts received in the two months after the year end.

In respect of this matter, select whether the audit junior should take no further action or refer to the supervisor.	▼

Picklist:

No further action
Refer to supervisor

Task 7.16

During the external audit of Bass Ltd, the audit junior identified three instances of sales receipts having been allocated to the wrong ledger account. The errors all occurred in August, when the sales ledger clerk was on holiday. No other such errors were found during testing.

In respect of this matter, select whether the audit junior should take no further action or refer to the supervisor.	▼

Picklist:

No further action
Refer to supervisor

Task 7.17

During the external audit of Snapper Ltd, whose year end is 31 December 20X4, the audit junior discovered, when verifying the bank statement, that many of the payments on that reconciliation did not clear the bank until near the end of January.

In respect of this matter, select whether the audit junior should take no further action or refer to the supervisor.	▼

Picklist:

No further action
Refer to supervisor

Chapter 8 Audit of liabilities (and related items)

Task 8.1

Identify whether the following statements in respect of the audit of trade payables are true or false by selecting the appropriate option.

Supplier statements provide excellent third party evidence about trade payables.		▼
Suppliers are circularised in the same way as receivables.		▼

Picklist:

True
False

....

Task 8.2

Which ONE of the following statements describes a situation when auditors are more likely to circularise payables?

When internal controls over purchases are weak and the auditor suspects that the trade payables balance has been understated. ☐

When internal controls over purchases are strong and the auditor suspects that the trade payables balance has been understated. ☐

When internal controls over purchases are weak and the auditor suspects that the trade payables balance has been overstated. ☐

When internal controls over purchases are strong and the auditor suspects that the trade payables balance has been overstated. ☐

....

Task 8.3

For each audit test below, match the test to the audit objective.

Audit objective	Audit test
Test completeness of purchases	
Test understatement of payables	

Picklist:

Trace sample of purchases from initial records to final accounts
Trace sample of purchases from final accounts to initial records
Reconcile purchase ledger with supplier statements
Reconcile purchase ledger with bank statements

Task 8.4

Which ONE of the following tests will auditors not carry out on the balance for accruals?

Recalculate the accruals

Verify accruals by reference to previous payments

Verify accruals by reference to subsequent payments

Compare accruals in current statement of comprehensive and prior years

Task 8.5

Which ONE of the following tests should not be carried out to determine the completeness of long-term liabilities?

Compare opening balances to the previous year's working papers
(closing balances at the end of last year)

Examine receipts for loan repayments

Compare balances to the general ledger

Review minutes and cashbook to ensure that all loans have been recorded

Task 8.6

During the audit of Mike's Motors Ltd, an audit junior performed a supplier statement reconciliation on a sample of trade payables balances at 31 May 20X3. Mike's Motors has good controls over goods inwards. There is some concern that Mike's Motors may be trying to reduce payables in the statement of financial position as it is trying to secure a loan. The audit junior has reconciled the balance on the purchase ledger in respect of Patel Engine Parts Ltd to the supplier statement as follows:

Patel Engine Parts Ltd

	£
Balance per supplier	37,600
Less: payment not on supplier statement	5,000
Less: invoice 1812 not recorded in ledger	5,400
Balance per purchase ledger	27,200

Identify which of the following accounting records each of the reconciling items must be verified to by selecting the appropriate option.

Payment not on supplier statement	▼
Invoice 1812	▼

Picklist: (for Payment not on supplier statement)

Bank statement
Cash book
Both bank statement and cash book

Picklist: (for Invoice 1812)

Purchase invoice
Purchase ledger
Both

Task 8.7

Kitchy Kabinets Ltd buys, sells and fits high quality kitchen furniture. Most of its suppliers are traditional craftsmen who do not operate the most efficient billing systems.

Set out, in a manner suitable for inclusion in the audit plan:

(i) **The risk associated with purchases cut off at Kitchy Kabinets Ltd**

(ii) **The objectives of year end cut-off procedures relating to the purchases system**

(iii) **The purchases year end cut-off tests you would carry out on the audit of Kitchy Kabinets Ltd**

Task 8.8

Johnny's Juices Ltd is an established juice bar which has very strong controls over its purchasing and inventory. It has two suppliers of juice, who represent 90% of the payables ledger and who do not usually send out supplier statements. The managing director, Johnny, who has a good relationship with the suppliers, requested supplier statements for the year end, to benefit his auditors, but the statements were not forthcoming. The company has an integrated computer system and can produce a high level of analysis about all aspects of operations. Your firm has audited Johnny's Juices Ltd for the last four years.

Set out, in a manner suitable for inclusion in the audit plan, the audit procedures to be undertaken in order to ensure that payables are fairly stated.

Task 8.9

During the external audit of Sturgeon Ltd, the audit junior noticed that a supplier had an incorrect VAT number. He tried the phone number on the invoice, but could not be connected. Sturgeon regularly purchases from the supplier but the total purchases are not material for the year. At the year end, the payables balance was zero.

In respect of this matter, select whether the audit junior should take no further action or should refer to the supervisor.	▼

Picklist:

No further action
Refer to supervisor

Task 8.10

The errors listed below were detected during the audit of payables at Mardens Ltd. Materiality is calculated at 5% of profit before tax. Profit before tax is £45,000. There were several errors detected during payables testing.

	£
Mispostings between supplier accounts	2,439
Invoices not posted in year re goods received in year	1,529
Payment not sent out until after year end	657

Identify whether the errors must be adjusted in order to issue an unmodified audit opinion on the financial statements by selecting the appropriate option.	▼

Picklist:

Must be adjusted
Do not need to be adjusted

Task 8.11

During the year, Tendosch Ltd entered into an agreement with a maintenance company to provide services to Tendosch Ltd for five years. The agreement was signed half way through the financial year. The total cost of the agreement is £60,000, with equal payments falling at the end of each year of the agreement.

Which ONE of the following balances should be included in the financial statements for the current year in respect of accruals in relation to this agreement?

£0 ☐

£6,000 ☐

£15,000 ☐

£60,000 ☐

Task 8.12

During the year ended 31 December 20X9, Anderson Ltd took out a bank loan which is repayable over the next five years. The terms of the loan state that there is nothing to pay for the first six months, and that then the loan will be paid off in £100 instalments on a monthly basis. The loan agreement was signed on 1 February. The audit junior has verified payments of £100 to the bank in August, September, October, November and December.

Identify the balance that should be included in the financial statements in each case by selecting the appropriate option.

Current liabilities	▼
Non current liabilities	▼

Picklist: (for Current liabilities)

£0
£500
£1,200

Picklist: (for Non-current liabilities)

£1,200
£3,700
£4,900

Chapter 9 Audit completion and reporting

Task 9.1

In respect of subsequent events, identify the auditors' duties to look for evidence.

	Duty	No duty
Before the auditor's report is signed	☐	☐
After the auditor's report is signed	☐	☐

Task 9.2

Identify whether the following statements in respect of written representations are true or false by selecting the appropriate option.

Written representations are the written evidence of everything the directors have said to auditors during the audit.	▼
Auditors are required to get written confirmation from the directors of their responsibilities with regard to the financial statements.	▼

Picklist:

True
False

Task 9.3

Set out the basic elements of the standard auditor's report.

Task 9.4

Below are two disagreements which have arisen in two separate audits. Both matters are material.

Identify which audit opinion will be given in each case by selecting the appropriate option.

The directors refuse to write off a debt owed by Sandicore Ltd, a company that has gone into liquidation.	▼
The auditors believe that the company is experiencing going concern issues. The directors have failed to disclose in the financial statements, claiming their recovery plan is going to get the company back on track. The auditors agree that the recovery plan has a high chance of success.	▼

Picklist:

Qualified
Adverse

Task 9.5

Set out the four possible types of opinion in an auditor's report where there are matters that affect the auditor's opinion and explain why each would arise.

Task 9.6

An audit junior has calculated some financial statement ratios to see if Glad Rags Limited's financial statements appear to make sense (given below).

The key figures from the statement of comprehensive income are sales revenue, which is £7,103,495, gross profit £2,121,814 and profit for the year £680,515.

Ratios		20X3
$\dfrac{\text{Gross profit}}{\text{Revenue}} \times 100$	$\dfrac{2,121,814}{7,103.495} \times 100 = 29.87\%$	(30.2%)
$\dfrac{\text{Profit for the year}}{\text{Revenue}} \times 100$	$\dfrac{680,515}{7,103,495} \times 100 = 9.58\%$	(9.52%)
$\dfrac{\text{Receivables}}{\text{Revenue}} \times 365$	$\dfrac{1,345,933}{7,103,495} \times 365 = 69 \text{ days}$	(67 days)
$\dfrac{\text{Payables}}{\text{Cost of sales}} \times 365$	$\dfrac{365,038}{4,981,681} \times 365 = 27 \text{ days}$	(28 days)

Identify whether the financial statements appear to make sense.	▼

Picklist:

Make sense
Do not make sense

Task 9.7

During the audit planning of The Glad Rags Limited, going concern was identified as a risk because:

(1) A major customer, BCS, is carrying out an audit of its suppliers
(2) The fact that Gladys Burton, the owner-manager is considering selling the company

Set out what particular matters should be considered in carrying out a going concern review.

Task 9.8

The audit work has been completed on the audit of Munstings Limited for the year ended 30 April 2X4. The audit senior has concluded that an unqualified auditor's opinion should be given.

Draft the relevant opinion paragraph.

Task 9.9

During the course of the audit work on inventory at Green Valleys Ltd, whose year end is 30 December, a material error was discovered. On 30 December a new recruit left a door to the plant room at one of the stores open overnight which meant that the heat regulation system failed and a large number of plants included in the inventory count at the year end died after the inventory count, and should have been written off. However, these plants have been included in inventory at full value (£67,495). The director does not wish to amend the financial statements as he insists that the inventory did exist at the year end and therefore it is fair to present that situation and recognise the loss on the inventory in the next financial year. Materiality is £65,000.

Identify whether the error needs to be adjusted or does not need to be adjusted to issue an unmodified audit opinion on the financial statements by selecting the appropriate option.	▼

Picklist:

Needs to be adjusted
Does not need to be adjusted

Task 9.10

For each of the following situations which have arisen in two unrelated audit clients, identify whether or not the audit opinion on the financial statements would be modified by selecting the appropriate option.

The auditors did not observe Handyco's inventory count at the year end, as they were not appointed until after that date. Due to the nature of the company's records, they have not been able to ascertain the existence of inventory by another method.	▼
The auditors did not observe Complicateco's inventory count due to staffing difficulties on the day. The company has detailed inventory records, and the auditors were able to attend the premises two days later and carry out test counts against the company's records. The company had maintained a record of inventory existing on the year end date and movements since are easy to trace through the system.	▼

Picklist:

Modified
Not modified

Chapter 10 Professional issues

Task 10.1

There is a difference between an auditor's legal relationship with the company being audited and other stakeholders.

Select the appropriate duty of care in each situation below.

The company being audited	▼
Individual shareholders in the company being audited	▼
The bank of the company being audited, who has given the company a substantial overdraft facility	▼

Picklist:

Duty of care is automatic
Duty of care must be proved
Duty of care cannot exist

Task 10.2

Auditors may use various methods of limiting their personal liability to clients.

Select the appropriate liability limitation method in each situation.

A contract stating the maximum sum an auditor is liable for, or the maximum proportion of liability an auditor will accept responsibility for.	▼
A legal entity which bears some similarity to a company and gives similar legal protection to members in respect of liability.	▼
Payments made to a third party to ensure a pay out to injured parties in the event of a negligence claim being successful.	▼

Picklist:

Limited liability partnership
Liability limitation agreement
Professional indemnity insurance

Task 10.3

You are the audit senior on the audit of Dowhop Limited, which will be commencing shortly. Your audit assistant is David Devley, who is new to the firm and has little experience of auditing. The owner of Dowhop Limited has discussed with the audit partner the possibility that she will seek to sell the business in the near future. No one else at the company is aware of her plans.

The audit manager has asked that you explain some fundamental aspects of auditing to David.

Compile brief notes for David's benefit explaining the following matters:

- **Working papers and what they should contain**

- **The auditor's duty of confidentiality**

- **How the audit team should treat the information about the owner's intentions when it attends the client to conduct the audit.**

Task 10.4

You are the auditor of a premiership football club of which you are also a fan. You have applied for a season ticket but there is a three-year waiting list.

One of the directors suggests that he can help you to jump the queue and if you make out a cheque for the season ticket, he will sort out a seat for you in the directors' box in time for the next home game.

Select the appropriate action.

The appropriate action is…	▼

Picklist:

Accept the director's offer
Decline the director's offer

Task 10.5

Attendance at inventory count is an accepted procedure for establishing the existence of inventories. Owing to pressure of work, you neglected to arrange for the physical observation of inventory at the premises of Leesmoor Ltd at 31 March 20X4, but your review of the instructions indicated that company procedures appeared to be in order. You decided to accept the amount at which inventory was stated in the financial statements at 31 March 20X4 on the grounds that:

(a) The instructions appeared to be satisfactory

(b) No problems had arisen in determining physical inventory quantities in previous years, and

(c) The figures in the financial statements generally 'made sense'.

You issued your unmodified audit report on 28 May 20X4 and without your knowledge or consent, Leesmoor used the financial statements and the auditor's report to obtain a material unsecured long-term loan from a third party. In October 20X4 the company was forced into liquidation and the long-term loan holder lost the amount of his loan. During the liquidation proceedings it became clear that inventory quantities at 31 March 20X4 had been considerably overstated.

Set out the probable legal position of your firm in respect of the above matter commenting specifically on the following:

(a) **The possibility of demonstrating your firm were negligent**

(b) **The fact that the inventory figure in the financial statements apparently 'made sense'**

(c) **The fact that you were not informed that the financial statements and your audit report were to be used to obtain additional finance.**

Task 10.6

During the audit of Multicorp plc, the audit senior identified a high number of consultancy payments in the statement of comprehensive income of a foreign subsidiary. On asking management to produce invoices in respect of the consultancy, management were unable to do so. Explanations as to the nature of the consultancy were sketchy. The audit senior believes that the consultancy payments represent bribes paid to government officials in the foreign country to ensure that Multicorp was able to build its factory and obtain certain licenses.

Which of the following is the correct action for the audit senior to take?

No action as such 'consultancy' is normal business practice in that country ☐

Report the matter to the board of directors of Multicorp ☐

Report the matter to the audit engagement partner ☐

Report the matter to the firm's Money Laundering Reporting Officer ☐

Task 10.7

Interview and listening skills are important tools for an external auditor. The auditor must apply professional scepticism when interviewing a client.

In a meeting with the audit partner, the financial controller of Truth Ltd started to mention to the audit partner that he was concerned that the management estimations of fair value in the financial statements were a little optimistic. However, at that point, the finance director entered the room and the financial controller stated that in his opinion assets had all been correctly valued.

Complete the following statement in respect of the reliability of the information provided by the financial controller by selecting the appropriate option.

The statement by the financial controller that assets had all been correctly valued is

[▼]

Picklist:

Likely to be reliable.
Not likely to be reliable.

Answer bank

Answer bank

External Auditing Answer Bank

Chapter 1

Task 1.1

Returns from customers and suppliers ☑

Task 1.2

An audit is an | examination | by an | independent qualified | examiner to ensure that the | financial statements | of a company, prepared from the accounting records by the | directors |, give a | true and fair view | of the company's affairs and transactions in the year.

Task 1.3

Private companies with a turnover of less than £6.5 million and a balance sheet total of less than £3.26 million are exempt from the requirement to have an audit.	True ▼
Public companies with a turnover of less than £6.5 million and a balance sheet total of less than £3.26 million are exempt from the requirement to have an audit.	False ▼ – a public company cannot qualify as small, and is therefore not exempt.
All companies for whom it has been unnecessary to record a transaction in the financial year are exempt from the requirement to have an audit.	False ▼ – dormant companies that are a bank/insurance company or a parent in a group must still be audited.

Task 1.4

	True	False
Companies must keep accounting records that are sufficient to disclose with **complete** accuracy at all times, the financial position of the company.	☐	✓ – the incorrect bits shown in bold.
Companies must keep accounting records that are sufficient to disclose with reasonable accuracy at the **company's accounting year end**, the financial position of the company.	☐	✓ – the incorrect bits shown in bold.
Companies must keep accounting records that are sufficient to disclose with reasonable accuracy at all times the financial position of the company.	✓	☐

Task 1.5

The advantages of having an audit include the following:

(a) Shareholders who are not involved in management gain reassurance from audited accounts about management's stewardship of the business.

(b) Audited accounts are a reliable source for a fair valuation of shares in an unquoted company either for taxation or other purposes.

(c) Some banks rely on accounts for the purposes of making loans and reviewing the value of security.

(d) Payables and potential payables can use audited accounts to assess the potential strength of the company.

(e) The audit provides management with an useful independent check on the accuracy of the accounting systems; the auditors can recommend improvements in those systems.

Task 1.6

The Financial Reporting Council (FRC) is an independent body that issues professional guidance for auditors to follow.	True	▼
The Government has delegated responsibility for standard setting and monitoring to the FRC.	True	▼
Auditors in the UK are required to follow the professional standards issued by the FRC.	True	▼
These standards are standards on how to audit, known as International Standards on Auditing (UK and Ireland) and Ethical Standards, which outline how auditors should behave and, in particular, how they should remain independent of their clients.	True	▼

Task 1.7

IAASB is committed to producing high quality audit standards and promoting international convergence in auditing practice.	True	▼
IAASB is a constituent body of the Financial Reporting Council (FRC), which is the independent regulator of accounting and auditing in the UK.	False	▼
When IAASB prepares new standards, it first researches the standard and drafts it, then subjects it to public comment, before issuing it after approval from 51% of the board.	False – at least 2/3rds of members must approve it.	▼

Task 1.8

The auditor does not examine each and every transaction in detail to ensure that it is correctly recorded and properly presented.	Reasonable assurance ▼
The view given in accounts is based on a combination of both fact and judgement and therefore cannot be characterised as either 'absolute' or 'correct'.	Reasonable assurance ▼
The financial statements should comply with expected standards and rules, for example, UK GAAP.	Fairness ▼

Task 1.9

The fact that accounting systems are subject to human error ☑

Task 1.10

Working papers are prepared by the external auditor because there is a professional requirement to do so.	True ▼
The primary reason for recording work in working papers is so that senior staff members can review junior staff members' work.	False ▼ – this is a subsidiary benefit.
Working papers should record contentious issues and how they were resolved.	True ▼

Task 1.11

An external audit conducted under International Standards on Auditing is

A reasonable assurance engagement ▼

Chapter 2

Task 2.1

The five components of an internal control system are:

Control environment, the entity's risk assessment process, information system, control activities and monitoring of controls.

Task 2.2

The control environment is the attitudes, awareness and actions of management and those charged with governance about internal control and its importance.	True	▼
If the directors follow control activities themselves and encourage others to do so, if they promote an attitude in a company that internal control is important, and encourage staff to monitor their own performance and the performance of others in observing control, then they can contribute to an excellent control environment.	True	▼
If directors override controls set up in a company and give other staff the impression that controls are not important, then they will be strongly contributing to a good control environment.	False	▼

Task 2.3

An information system that is heavily documented in physical ledgers.	Manual	▼
A system which is retained predominantly in electronic format.	Computerised	▼

Task 2.4

Control activities

A company will not place an order for goods until a senior member of staff has confirmed that order.	Information processing ▼
A company locks the storeroom so that raw materials cannot be accessed.	Physical controls ▼
An accounts department is organised so that Debbie is in charge of invoicing and Phil is in charge of receipts.	Segregation of duties ▼

Task 2.5

	Strong	Weak
Directors document control policies and procedures and communicate them to all staff.	✓	
Directors demand staff push themselves to obtain goals and promote the concept of 'by any means possible'.		✓ – this attitude implies controls may be overridden to achieve results.
A director has perpetrated a fraud.		✓ – control environment is about the attitudes, actions and awareness of high level staff.

Task 2.6

	Reliance	No reliance
A company where there is an internal audit function which monitors controls on a systematic and regular basis.	✓	☐
A small company where the owner-manager has virtual control over all accounting transactions, aided by his part-time, unqualified wife.	☐	✓

Task 2.7

Customers do not pay for the goods.	Risk ▼
Customers should pay promptly for goods.	Control objective ▼
Customers are allocated credit limits.	Control procedure ▼

Task 2.8

A company intends to invoice all despatches correctly.	Control objective ▼
A company can match despatch records with invoices prior to invoices being sent out.	Control procedure ▼
A company can send out goods and not invoice them.	Risk ▼

Task 2.9

Company pays for goods it has not received.	Risk ▼
Company only accepts goods it has ordered.	Control objective ▼
Company compares invoices to purchase orders and GRNs	Control procedure ▼

Task 2.10

Controls present

- Necessity for orders is evidenced prior to ordering and a requisition is raised
- The company has a policy for choosing suppliers
- Goods received are examined for quantity and quality
- Goods received are checked against the order
- Supplier invoices are checked to the order
- Supplier invoices are checked for prices, quantities and calculations and given a reference number
- Purchases are entered on the purchase ledger promptly
- Cheque requests are presented for approval with supporting documentation
- Supplier statements are reconciled to the purchase ledger
- The purchase ledger control account is regularly reconciled with the purchase ledger list of balances

Task 2.11

A company wants to pay the right amount for goods purchased.	Control objective ▼
A company reconciles supplier statements to the purchase ledger.	Control procedure ▼
A company may pay for goods which are used for personal purposes.	Risk ▼

Task 2.12

The company should pay employees for work done.	Control objective ▼
The company could make incorrect payments to HMRC.	Risk ▼
The company reviews payroll against budgets.	Control procedure ▼

Task 2.13

The company buys assets it does not need.	Risk	▼
Depreciation rates should reflect the useful life of an asset.	Control objective	▼
The company keeps a non current assets register.	Control procedure	▼

Task 2.14

Goods inwards are checked and recorded.	Control procedure	▼
Goods may be used for personal gain.	Risk	▼
Goods are available when required for use in the business.	Control objective	▼

Task 2.15

Controls may be too expensive to operate on a daily basis ✓

Task 2.16

The payroll clerk and the human resources manager, who authorises the payroll on a monthly basis, are working together to defraud the company by benefiting from the salaries of two false employees.	Collusion	▼
Sales made to Dixie, a major customer, are always processed at a special discount not recognised by the computer controls, so the sales director always has to process Dixie's sales, and 'fix' the problem.	Management override	▼

Task 2.17

Internal control procedure	Risk mitigated
Credit checks run on new customers.	Customers are not good credit risks.
Despatches are checked for quality before leaving the warehouse.	Customers are issued credit notes incorrectly.

Task 2.18

Risk	Internal control procedure to mitigate.
Company pays for poor quality goods.	Company reviews all goods inwards for condition.
Company pays for the same invoice twice.	Company records payments promptly on the purchases ledger.

Chapter 3

Task 3.1

A Graph ☑

Auditors may record systems by using:

- Narrative notes
- Flowcharts
- Internal control questionnaires

Task 3.2

A walkthrough test is a test designed to ensure that the system ⬚operates⬚ as the ⬚auditors⬚ have been told that it does. They select a transaction in a particular area (for example, a sale or a purchase) and trace it through the company's information system from the initial point (for example, the sales ⬚order⬚, or the purchase ⬚requisition⬚).

Task 3.3

Question	Yes/No	Comment
Are orders only accepted from low credit risks?	Yes	Sales staff check that customers have not exceeded limits.
Are despatches checked by appropriate personnel?	Yes	Ian Jones checks order prior to despatch.
Are goods sent out recorded?	Yes	Ian Jones raises a despatch note.
Are customers required to give evidence of receipt of goods?	Yes	They are requested to sign a copy of the despatch note.
Are invoices checked to despatch notes and invoices?	Yes	The order and despatch note are matched prior to invoicing.
Are invoices prepared using authorised prices?	Yes	The sales department have completed authorised prices on the order. Jane does not appear to carry out additional checks on invoices.
Are invoices checked to ensure they add up correctly?	No	Jane does not appear to carry out additional checks on invoices.
Are sales receipts matched with invoices?	No	No. Receipts are simply posted to the ledger and cashbook.
Are statements sent out regularly?	Yes	Monthly
Are overdue accounts reviewed regularly?	No	No review appears to take place, but bad debts are rare.

Question	Yes/No	Comment
Are there safeguards over post received to ensure that cheques are not intercepted?	No	Post is opened elsewhere and transferred to the accounts department.
Are bankings made daily?	No	However, cheques are kept securely until they are banked.
Would it be appropriate to perform tests of control in this area? (Give reason/reasons in the comments box.)	Yes	There appears to be a good system of control over ordering, despatch, invoicing and recording. Substantive tests should also be carried out over receipts and bad debts where controls are weakest.

Task 3.4

Sales revenue, payroll, cash ☑

Task 3.5

	True	False
The auditor may take a combined approach, where he will test controls and then reduce his subsequent substantive testing (although he must always carry out tests of detail on material items).	☑	☐
The auditor may take a substantive approach, where he does not test controls, but instead renders control risk as high and conducts more tests of detail instead.	☑	☐

Task 3.6

	Reliance	No-reliance
The directors of LightLynx Ltd demand close attention to control procedures, and they monitor how the system is operating on a monthly basis.	☑	☐
At Simlaglow Ltd, there is an accounting staff of two, the financial controller, and his assistant.	☐	☑ – there are insufficient staff for adequate segregation of duties.
There are ten people in the accounts department at Luxicon Ltd. The financial controller keeps a close interest in all transactions, and often intervenes to speed up proceedings.	☐	☑ – there is a suggestion of management override of controls here.

Task 3.7

Selection of a sample of sales ledger accounts over £30,000.	Audit software	▼
Input of sales invoices with false customer numbers to ensure application controls function correctly.	Test data	▼
Analytical procedures on statement of comprehensive income, on a line by line approach.	Audit software	▼

Task 3.8

Management communicate controls values to staff and ensure new staff are thoroughly training in controls procedures.	Strong ▼
Management emphasise the importance of targets over procedures.	Weak ▼
Management include adherence to company procedures in annual appraisals for staff members.	Strong ▼

Task 3.9

	Strength	Weakness
Julie raises the sales invoices on the basis of the goods received notes she is sent by the warehouse. She inputs the information, prints the invoices, and sends them out.	☐	✓ – she does not check the invoices prior to sending to check they are correct.
Statements are sent to customers on a monthly basis.	✓	☐

Task 3.10

Weakness: invoicing

Weakness: receipts

- Post opening appears to be unsupervised and no initial list of receipts is made.
- Customer remittances do not appear to be retained.

(i) **Consequences**

- Receipts could be lost or stolen on arrival at the company.

(ii) **Recommendations**

- Ideally, someone from the accounts department should attend the opening of the post and make an initial list of receipts.
- Customer remittances should be retained so that receipts can be reconciled to specific invoices.

Note: based on the information available at the time this book was written, we anticipate a task like this would be human marked in the real assessment.

Task 3.11

Tests of controls

Controls	Tests of control
The company has a policy for choosing suppliers	Review a sample of orders – to ensure that the suppliers appear on the approved list.
Goods received are examined for quantity and quality	Observe the stores manager receiving some goods – to ensure that they are examined properly.
Goods received are checked against the order	Observe the stores manager receiving some goods – to ensure he checks the order. Review a sample of orders – to see if he has noted the check (by initialling for example).

Task 3.12

Tests of controls

Controls	Tests of control
Hours worked are recorded	Review clockcards – they are evidence of hours being recorded
Hours worked are reviewed	Review clockcards – to look for evidence of authorisation
Payroll is prepared by director	Review payroll – to check that it is indeed prepared by the director.

Task 3.13

Present system

No passwords are required to access any part of the computerised accounting system.

Consequences

Unrestricted access to the computer system could lead to error, deliberate alteration of accounting records, inefficiency and possible fraud.

Recommendation

Your present software includes the facility to allow restricted access to systems by your staff through a structured system of passwords that can be changed frequently.

We recommend that passwords should be introduced as soon as possible.

Present system

Whilst security backup copies of files are taken, these copies are kept in the desk occupied by the accounts clerk.

Consequences

Files may be lost, damaged or accessed without authorisation.

Recommendation

We recommend that backup files are stored securely, for example, in a fire-proof safe.

Note: based on the information available at the time this book was written, we anticipate a task like this would be human marked in the real assessment.

Task 3.14

Sandra reconciles supplier statements with the purchase ledger as she receives them.	Strength ▼
Payments, which are approved by a director, are made on a monthly basis on the basis of a printout of due items from the purchase ledger.	Strength ▼

Task 3.15

Each member of staff is allocated a personnel file on arrival, which is updated for any changes in pay rates or hours.	Strength ▼
The payroll is created by the wages clerk on the last Thursday of a month. She runs the payroll package which automatically produces a bank payments list and notifies the bank to pay the salaries.	Weakness ▼ – the payroll does not appear to be authorised by a senior member of staff.

Task 3.16

	Strength	Weakness
The company maintains a non current asset register. The operations manager checks the register to physical assets once a year.	✓	☐
The operations manager and the purchasing director meet monthly to discuss asset requirements for the business.	✓	☐

Task 3.17

Inventory is kept in a locked store, secured by the key card system in operation at the company. All members of staff are issued with key cards.	Weakness ▼ – the inventory is available to any staff member unnecessarily. Access should be restricted.
The production manager reviews levels of inventory and makes requisitions on a monthly basis.	Weakness ▼ – needful inventory could run out during a month and cause business interruption. The company should have reorder levels which trigger requisition.

Task 3.18

Central list of suppliers not used

(i) **Consequences**

Using non-approved suppliers might result in the following problems:

- Less favourable terms for the business (for example, credit terms, leading to cash flow problems)

- Lower quality goods being purchased leading to problems in production

- Less reliable delivery leading to problems in production

(ii) **Recommendations**

- As there seems to be a team in the purchasing department at Miraglow, I would recommend that deals that seem to be good value to the company are referred to a nominated member of staff.

- This individual can investigate whether all aspects of the deal are likely to benefit Miraglow and obtain references/check credentials of the company, and then notify the directors to get approval for using the new supplier, rather than using lots of different suppliers on an ad hoc basis.

Note: based on the information available at the time this book was written, we anticipate a task like this would be human marked in the real assessment.

···

Task 3.19

The identification of a fraud, relating to an material monetary amount, carried out by a director of the audited entity, which was not prevented by the entity's internal control system.

Significant deficiency ▼

···

Chapter 4

Task 4.1

Auditors are required to obtain an understanding of the entity and its environment only when the client is a new client.	False	▼
Auditors are required to obtain an understanding of the entity and its environment so that they are able to assess the risks relating to the audit.	True	▼

Task 4.2

Audit risk is the risk that the auditors give an inappropriate opinion on the financial statements. It is made up of three components:

- **Inherent** ▼ risk – risks arising as a result of the nature of the business, its transactions and environment
- **Control** ▼ risk – the risk that the control system at the company does not detect, correct or prevent misstatements

  (These two risks combined are the risk that misstatements will exist in the financial statements in the first place)
- **Detection** ▼ risk – the risk that auditors do not discover misstatements in the financial statements

Task 4.3

(4) Identify detection risk as part of a review of audit firm procedure ✓

Detection risk is not so much identified as calculated based on the risk of material misstatement identified at the client. It is specific to the particular audit.

The auditor will take the following steps:

(1) Identify inherent and control risks while obtaining an understanding of the entity
(2) Relate identified risks to what could go wrong at a financial statement level
(3) Consider if the risks are so big they could cause material misstatement

Task 4.4

At a financial statement level:

- Items can be understated or overstated
- Items requiring disclosure can be omitted

....

Task 4.5

	True	False
Materiality is the concept of importance to users.	☑	☐
It is relevant to auditors because they will only test items which are material.	☐	☑ – materiality contributes to sample selection but some immaterial items will be tested to ensure that overall the financial statements are materially fairly stated.
Calculating materiality and selecting samples on the basis of materiality helps the auditor to reduce audit risk to an acceptable level.	☑ – this is the relationship between materiality and audit risk.	☐

....

Task 4.6

A transaction in the normal course of business for the entity   ☑

This does not suggest a significant risk – a significant risk might be indicated by a transaction outside the normal course of business for an entity.

....

Task 4.7

This answer gives three risks rather than two, to show the range of answers that you might have given

Audit risk	Potential impact on financial statements
Company relies heavily on two customers. One of the customers is currently reviewing Glad Rags to ensure it meets the required qualities of being a quality supplier.	Going concern issues if the company were to lose this custom.
Company relies heavily on the involvement of the sole director, Gladys, who is considering selling the company.	Dominance of an individual director can reduce effectiveness of internal control systems, which could cause error throughout the financial statements. Gladys' plans to sell the company could have implications for going concern, if she does not find a buyer for the company. Gladys' plans to sell the company could lead to a desire to bias the financial statements so that the company looks like a good investment.
The control system is restricted by the low number of administrative staff involved and there appears to be limited segregation of duties in the accounts department.	Lack of segregation of duties can result in errors not being detected by the control systems and therefore arising anywhere in the financial statements. This would cast concern particularly on sales revenue/receivables and purchases/payables, which are all likely to be material balances.

Task 4.8

The company issues inventory to customers on a sale or return basis.	Assets could be over- or understated ▼ – because the company might forget to include inventory which is at the third party, or might include inventory that the third party has actually sold.
The non current asset register is not reconciled regularly with the actual assets.	Assets could be over- or understated ▼ – because assets might be missing or obsolete, or assets might have been bought and not included in the register.

Task 4.9

	Increase	Reduce
The company operates in a highly regulated industry.	✓	☐
The company has an internal audit function committed to monitoring internal controls.	☐	✓
The company has set ambitious growth targets for all its salesmen, to be judged at the end of the financial year.	✓	☐

Task 4.10

	Increase	Decrease
The role of sales ledger clerk has been filled by four different people during the year, following the retirement of a long-standing sales ledger clerk at the end of last year.	✓	☐
The financial controller is a qualified accountant, as are two of his high level staff.	☐	✓
The directors have a positive attitude towards controls and enforce them company-wide.	☐	✓

Task 4.11

A control such as a [**password** ▼] may [**prevent** ▼] unauthorised access to a computer programme so that errors cannot be deliberately input.

Alternatively a control such as a reconciliation [**detects** ▼] mistakes, which the person carrying out the reconciliation can then [**correct** ▼], so that there is no misstatement in the financial statements as a result.

Task 4.12

Material and pervasive is taken to mean that the misstatement is:

- **Not confined** ▼ to one item in the financial statements

- **Confined** ▼ to one item, but the item could represent a substantial portion of the financial statements

- If relating to a disclosure, **fundamental** ▼ to users' understanding of the financial statements.

Chapter 5

Task 5.1

The audit strategy is the overall approach for carrying out the audit.	True ▼
The audit plan contains detailed instructions for testing each audit area.	True ▼

Task 5.2

Whether the audit should be accepted by the firm ☑

This will already have been decided previously.

Task 5.3

An auditor needs to obtain sufficient, appropriate evidence.	True ▼
Sufficient means evidence from at least two sources.	False ▼

Task 5.4

	Test of control	Substantive procedure
Observation of inventory count	☑	☐
Inspection of an invoice to vouch cost of new non current asset	☐	☑
Recalculation of depreciation charge	☐	☑

Task 5.5

Non current assets	Analytical procedures ▼
Inventory	Tests of details ▼
Receivables	Tests of details ▼
Bank	Analytical procedures ▼
Payables	Tests of details ▼

The following items will require testing because they are above the materiality limit (£70,000):

- Inventory
- Receivables
- Payables falling due in less than one year

However, non current assets and cash should also be reviewed in case they contain an error of understatement which is material.

Task 5.6

Non current assets	Tests of details ▼
Inventory	Tests of details ▼
Receivables	Analytical procedures ▼
Bank	Tests of details ▼
Trade payables	Tests of details ▼
Accruals	Analytical procedures ▼
Bank loan	Tests of details ▼

The following balances are material and should be tested in detail:

- Non current assets
- Inventory
- Trade payables
- Bank loan

In addition, the bank balance has gone into overdraft which is a major difference from last year. This balance should also be tested in detail, although it is immaterial.

The receivables balance and the accruals balances are immaterial and have not changed significantly from the previous year, therefore it should only be tested by analytical procedures.

Task 5.7

Financial statement assertion	Example test
Completeness	(a) Review of events after the end of the reporting period (b) Cut off (c) Analytical procedures (d) Confirmations (e) Reconciliations to control account (f) Sequence checks (g) Review of reciprocal populations
Rights and obligations	(a) Checking invoices for proof that item belongs to the company (b) Confirmations with third parties
Cut-off	(a) Match up last GRNs with purchase invoices to ensure liability is recorded in the correct period (b) Match up last GDNs with sales invoices to ensure income is recorded in the correct period
Valuation	(a) Checking invoices (b) Recalculation (c) Confirming accounting policy consistent and reasonable (d) Review of post period end payments and invoices
Existence	(a) Physical verification (b) Third party confirmations (c) Cut off testing
Occurrence	(a) Inspection of supporting documentation (b) Confirmation from directors that transactions relate to business (c) Inspection of items purchased
Accuracy	(a) Re-calculation of correct amounts (b) Third party confirmation (c) Expert valuation (d) Analytical procedures
Classification/understandability	(a) Check compliance with Companies Act and accounting standards

Task 5.8

Auditor intends to increase his reliance on tests of controls.	Increase ▼
Auditor is selecting a sample of sales invoices, when a new customer means the volume of sales at the client has increased by 20%.	No effect ▼
Auditors' tolerable deviation rate rises from 1.5% to 2%.	Decrease ▼

Task 5.9

Obtain evidence of the completeness of the trade payables balance.	Purchase requisition
Obtain evidence that the bank balance is fairly stated.	Bank letter

Task 5.10

Sales revenue has increased by 3% but the gross profit margin is down by 1.5%.	More information required to draw a conclusion ▼
Sales in the last month of the year were 5% higher than in previous years, and also 4% higher than the average for a month for the company.	Sales revenue may be overstated ▼

Task 5.11

When sampling, the auditor must ensure that all sampling items have an equal chance of selection.	True ▼
When an auditor selects a sample of invoices at random from the filed invoices for the year, this is known as the random approach to sampling.	False ▼ – this is haphazard selection.

Task 5.12

Description on the invoice.	Classification ▼
Date on the invoice.	Cut off ▼

Task 5.13

	Test of control	Substantive procedure
A test to verify the operation of procedures designed to safeguard the business.	✓	☐
A comparison of financial and non-financial information by the auditor.	☐	✓ (analytical procedure)
A test to verify an assertion made in the financial statements.	☐	✓

Chapter 6

Task 6.1

The inventory count ☑

Task 6.2

The company records a sale but the inventory is also counted as existing at the year end.	(i) Profit is overstated
	(ii) Assets are overstated
The company accepts goods on the day of the inventory count, which get included in the count, but do not record the invoice in purchases until the following year.	(i) Profit is overstated
	(ii) Liabilities are understated

Task 6.3

The auditors will need to verify:

- The initial cost of the raw materials (usually tested by reference to original purchase invoices)

- The cost of conversion to finished goods (for example, labour costs, usually tested by reference to time records and the payroll, and overhead costs, usually tested by reference to overall overhead costs and the invoices for these costs)

Task 6.4

Review sales prices during the year to ensure that none have been significantly low. It is the value of items at the year end that the auditors are concerned with. ☑

Task 6.5

Inventory count – key issues

I must review the count instructions and ensure that the count is carried out in accordance with them.

I must test-check some of the counts that the checkers have made. Last year's sample was 12. As Joe Worple has stated that there are no major changes in inventory this year, the same sample size should be used.

I will focus my attention on raw materials, which is likely to be a higher amount in total than finished goods. In particular, I should ensure that I include within my count the specialist fabric A001, and the major inventory lines of S01, CJ02 and CJ03. Given that the stores manager has said there are no major changes in inventory, these items should be high value as they were last year.

I should also select some finished goods within the sample as the overall value of finished goods may be higher than raw materials, although the quantity is smaller and ensure that, as instructed, no work in progress exists.

I should remeasure some items during the count to ensure that the controls over amount of fabric operate effectively. I suggest an initial sample of 5 bales. I should also review a sample of the records on the bales to ensure that they are arithmetically accurate.

The main count will be taking place in the stores, so I will meet Mr Worple there. However, I will also ensure that I attend the machine room at 3pm to ensure that all operations have finished before the count starts.

Lastly, I should obtain details of the last delivery from the factory and the last delivery to the factory before the count to enable inventory cut off tests to be carried out at the final audit.

Review of count instructions

The instructions show that the count has been well thought out and appears organised. There are good controls over checks and to ensure that items are not counted twice. Controls to prevent movements of inventory during the count appear to be sound. Provided the count is carried out according to the instructions, the count should be capable of providing a suitable figure for inventory existence.

The key control is the existing control over quantity of inventory, which is that the bales are marked down for fabric removed and most of it is not remeasured at the count. We must be satisfied that this control is operating effectively to be able to rely on the count. Therefore it is important to check both that the record attached to the inventory tallies with the amount of inventory present and that the records are arithmetically accurate.

Note: based on the information available at the time this book was written, we anticipate a task like this would be human marked in the real assessment.

Task 6.6

Identify the appropriate conclusion to draw about inventory cut off at this stage by selecting the appropriate option.	Cut off is fairly stated ▼

An error was discovered in purchase cut off. One invoice, value £2,476, was included in December purchases in error. This is not material, but should be included on a schedule of non-material potential adjustments.

· ·

Task 6.7

Identify which of the tests needs to be carried out to draw a conclusion as to whether the existence of inventory is fairly stated by selecting the appropriate option.	Trace test count items to final inventory sheets ▼

· ·

Task 6.8

(i) Risks

- Damaged raw materials may be valued too high
- Raw materials may be valued inappropriately
- The level and percentage completion of WIP at count date may be miscalculated
- Inventory for customer in financial difficulties may be obsolete (unless it is suitably non specific to be sold to other parties)

(ii) Procedures relating to valuation

At inventory count

- Identify and record damaged inventory and potentially obsolete inventory
- Identify WIP and assess degree of completion

At final audit

- Ensure items noted at inventory count included in final inventory sheets
- Ensure obsolete items assigned no or suitably reduced value
- Verify costs of sample of raw materials to appropriate invoices for accounting method
- Consider whether accounting method for cost appropriate for raw materials
- Verify costs of WIP to payroll and overhead documentation such as purchase invoices

- Assess whether appropriate percentage completeness has been calculated for cost
- Review business after the year end with troubled customer (check sales orders/invoices/receipts) to see if inventory was sold/paid for and should be valued in financial statements
- Perform general NRV review of sales in next year

Note: based on the information available at the time this book was written, we anticipate a task like this would be human marked in the real assessment.

Task 6.9

FG135933 and X1369443 only

Task 6.10

Audit procedures

Existence – controls

- Attend a scheduled count (any of the four in the year)
- Ensure count instructions suggest controls over count are good
- Ensure count instructions are followed
- Ensure only goods that should be counted are counted
- Ensure that inventory movements are minimised during the count

Existence – substantive

- Attend the company on 31 December and test count a sample of inventory items from inventory records to actual inventory and vice versa.

- Ensure that a list of inventory on hand on 31 December is retained for the purposes of the final audit.

Completeness

- Select a sample of goods in before and after yearend (per inventory records) and trace to purchase ledger to ensure that the purchases are recorded in the same period as the goods in.

- Select a sample of goods out before and after the yearend (per inventory records) and trace to the sales ledger to ensure that sales are recorded in the same period as goods out.

Note: based on the information available at the time this book was written, we anticipate a task like this would be human marked in the real assessment.

Chapter 7

Task 7.1

Inspect assets to see if they are in use and good condition – a test for existence/valuation ✓

Task 7.2

Review depreciation rates for reasonableness (given asset lives, residual values, replacement policy, possible obsolescence)	Valuation ▾
Vouch title deeds of buildings.	Rights and obligations ▾
Inspect a sample of assets listed in the non current asset register.	Existence ▾

Task 7.3

Client: Kandistors Limited	**Prepared by:**
Year-end: 31 December 20X3	**Reviewed by:**
Subject: Non current assets	**Date: Date:**

Objective	Test		Completed by
Completeness	1	Ensure **opening balances** in **accounting records agree to last year's accounts.**	
	2	**Check** that the **assets seen** at the client's premises have been **recorded** in **the non current asset register.**	
	3	**Compare** the **non current asset register** with the **non current asset accounts** in the ledger, and check that **differences** in **value** can be **satisfactorily explained.**	
	4	**Review repairs, maintenance** and **sundry expenditure** during the year, and **enquire** into **any expenditure** that looks as if it should have been **capitalised.**	

Objective	Test		Completed by
	5	Compare actual **non current asset expenditure** with **budgeted expenditure** and **obtain explanations** for differences.	
	6	**Check** that all **non current asset expenditure** shown as authorised in the board minutes has been made.	
Existence	1	**Inspect a sample of assets** that are **recorded** in the non current **asset register.**	
	2	**Examine invoices** for **smaller furniture and equipment additions** to see if any have been **incorrectly capitalised.**	
Ownership	1	**Inspect title deeds** for land and buildings.	
	2	**Inspect other documentation** (vehicle registration documents, insurance policies) for evidence of title to other assets.	
	3	Inspect **purchase invoices,** records of **assets received** and **solicitors' completion statements** for **assets purchased** during the year to see if they are in the client's name and purchases have been properly authorised.	
	4	**Review bank letter** for details of assets and title documents held.	
Valuation	1	When inspecting assets, note any **signs of undue wear** or **lack of use.**	
	2	**Examine purchase invoices** for evidence of costs of assets purchased during the year.	

Note: based on the information available at the time this book was written, we anticipate a task like this would be human marked in the real assessment.

Task 7.4

All of them ☑

Valuation ▼

Task 7.5

	True	False
Auditors often perform analytical procedures when auditing sales revenue as there is usually a great deal of analytical information about sales revenue (for example, analyses of sales per month or per product) at a company, and sales revenue has a number of predictable relationships (with receivables, with gross margin) so it is a good balance to test by analytical procedures.	✓	☐
Auditors may test understatement of sales revenue by tracing a sale from the general ledger back through the system to the sales order.	☐	✓ – understatement is tested by starting with source documents (for example, sales orders).

Task 7.6

Bank letter requests should be made by the ...	Auditors ▼
Bank letter requests should be sent to the bank ...	A month before the year end ▼

Task 7.7

Window dressing ▼ is the practice of manipulating when cash receipts and payments are recorded and sent out to manipulate **statement of financial position** ▼ results at the year end.

For example, if a company wanted liabilities to look **lower** ▼ , then it might record a number of payments (which would also therefore be included on the bank reconciliation, reducing the bank balance) but not physically send those cheques out until after the year end, so that in practice, the bank balance is **higher** ▼ than it appears to be in the accounts, as is the **payables** ▼ balance.

Task 7.8

(i)	BCS difference	Bank statements
(ii)	Tisco stores difference	Goods returned note

Task 7.9

Audit of valuation of receivables

Valuation of receivables can be tested by scrutinising the cash paid subsequent to the year end. Auditors will be particularly concerned with older receivables on the ledger, especially when subsequent receivables have been paid, as this may indicate that the old receivable is not likely to be paid and has therefore been overvalued.

Audit procedures:

(1) Obtain an aged receivable analysis from the sales ledger at 30 November

(2) Scrutinise it to identify receivables greater than 60 days old at 30 November (60 days being the standard payment period of Glad Rags' customers)

(3) Review the cash book for evidence of the old receivables being paid

(4) If some old receivables are still unpaid as at the middle of January, they must be discussed with the accountant to assess whether action has been taken

(5) Scrutinise any correspondence with the late payer

(6) Consider any allowance made for irrecoverable debts and assess whether it is sufficient

(7) Identify any further adjustments that might need to be made in respect of irrecoverable debts and write them on the schedule of unadjusted errors

Note: based on the information available at the time this book was written, we anticipate a task like this would be human marked in the real assessment.

Task 7.10

Tests to be carried out on non current assets at Craftys:

Completeness

- Compare non current assets in the general ledger with the non current asset register and reconcile any differences

- Select a sample of assets which physically exist and trace them to the non current asset register

- Review sensitive balances in the statement of comprehensive income (such as repairs or motor costs) to ensure items which should have been capitalised have not been expensed in the year

Rights and obligations

- Review title deeds for land and buildings
- Check a sample of registration documents for company vehicles

Existence

- Select a sample of assets from the non current asset register and trace the physical assets

- Inspect the assets to ensure they exist, and are in good condition and use

Valuation

As assets have not been revalued, focus valuation testing on additions.

- Check the purchase invoices for the new vehicles and fittings
- Review depreciation rates to ensure they are reasonable
- Recalculate depreciation to ensure it has been correctly calculated
- Ensure value of major land and buildings assets has not been impaired

Note: based on the information available at the time this book was written, we anticipate a task like this would be human marked in the real assessment.

●●

Task 7.11

Shop 1 sales income is £2,521,634	Appear reasonable ▼
Cafe sales income is £431,996	Appear reasonable ▼
Total sales income £5,673,676	Understated ▼

●●

Task 7.12

Post year end bank statements ☑

....

Task 7.13

Risks

- It is possible that at planning date Diversity Ltd is in arrears for its first payment owed to Carl Ltd, although depending on the exact timings of invoices, as Diversity only became a customer in the last quarter, it may not quite be.

- Diversity is a new customer with no history with Carl, and there is a risk that despite the credit checks that were carried out (and as Diversity is a new company, these may not have been very detailed) that Diversity is a bad credit risk and its debt will be overstated in the financial statements.

- This is backed up by speculation in the press that the company does not have the working capital to sustain operations.

- In addition, Carl Ltd's staff have requested that we do not seek direct confirmation of Diversity's balance, which restricts our audit work, and could mean, particularly in the absence of a payment pattern that it is difficult to obtain audit evidence in this area.

- This could lead to there being a limitation in scope on our audit (as we are being prevented from obtaining evidence that would normally be available to us). However, if Diversity continue to be in arrears and we explain the seriousness to us of a lack of direct evidence, it is likely that the company will contact Diversity on our behalf (particularly since if the situation perpetuates itself, the credit controller will have to contact Diversity to request payment of the debt).

Procedures

- Review sales ledger receipts subsequent to audit planning date to see if Diversity have paid the balance or established a payment pattern (for example, a significant proportion of the debt may have been paid by the time of the audit).

- Discuss Diversity's failure to keep to their credit terms with Carl Ltd's credit controller to see if she has had discussions and/or correspondence with the customer.

- Review correspondence if any

- Corroborate any matters referred to in correspondence (for example, credits requested/credit notes)

- Consider whether an allowance is required if receivable appears irrecoverable.

Note: based on the information available at the time this book was written, we anticipate a task like this would be human marked in the real assessment.

....

Task 7.14

£33,000 ☑

The replacement engine and the new software both sound like capital items.

Task 7.15

In respect of this matter, select whether the audit junior should take no further action or refer to the supervisor.	Refer to supervisor ▼ – this could be indication of a fraud being carried out by the sales ledger clerk.

Task 7.16

In respect of this matter, select whether the audit junior should take no further action or refer to the supervisor.	No further action ▼

Task 7.17

In respect of this matter, select whether the audit junior should take no further action or refer to the supervisor.	Refer to supervisor ▼ – the company may have been attempting to manipulate the statement of financial position.

Chapter 8

Task 8.1

Supplier statements provide excellent third party evidence about trade payables.	True ▼
Suppliers are circularised in the same way as receivables.	False ▼ – in fact this is rare, because supplier statements provide excellent evidence.

Task 8.2

When internal controls over purchases are weak and the auditor suspects that the trade payables balance has been understated. ☑

Task 8.3

Audit objective	Audit test
Test completeness of purchases	Trace sample of purchases from initial records to final accounts
Test understatement of payables	Reconcile purchase ledger with supplier statements

Task 8.4

Verify accruals by reference to previous payments ☑

Task 8.5

Examine receipts for loan repayments (valuation) ☑

Task 8.6

Payment not on supplier statement	Both bank statement and cash book ▼ – the cash book will give evidence that the payment was made through the books prior to the year end. The auditor will also wish to ensure that the payment cleared early in May (ie that the timing of the payment is genuine).
Invoice 1812	Purchase invoice ▼ – this should have the GRN attached to it as controls are good. The date of goods receipt determines whether there is a liability at year end date.

Task 8.7

Risk: Suppliers might be slow in submitting their invoices and therefore it may be difficult to ensure that all liabilities at the year end are recorded in the correct period.

Objectives: The key audit objective is to ensure that all relevant liabilities are recorded in the correct period.

Procedures: A standard purchase cut-off test would be to take a sample of goods received notes for an appropriate period before the year end and after the year end and trace these to suppliers' invoices and payables records and the purchase ledger to confirm that the relevant liabilities are taken up in the correct year.

Note: based on the information available at the time this book was written, we anticipate a task like this would be human marked in the real assessment.

Task 8.8

Payables testing at Johnny's Juices Ltd

- Obtain payables ledger listing and check for arithmetical accuracy
- Perform analytical procedures on payables balance (compare with prior years)
- If there are unexpected fluctuations, request monthly purchases information and ensure it ties in with sales patterns
- If analytical procedures do not provide satisfactory evidence concerning payables balance, it may be necessary to reconstruct year end balance by reviewing invoices and payment records

Note: based on the information available at the time this book was written, we anticipate a task like this would be human marked in the real assessment.

Task 8.9

In respect of this matter, select whether the audit junior should take no further action or should refer to the supervisor.	Refer to supervisor ▼ – the supplier may be fake suggesting a fraud being carried out in the purchase ledger.

Task 8.10

Identify whether the errors must be adjusted in order to issue an unmodified audit opinion on the financial statements by selecting the appropriate option.	Do not need to be adjusted ▼ – the first error should not be projected against the total as they do not affect the total balance. The other two are less than 5% of profit before tax.

Task 8.11

£6,000 ✓

Task 8.12

Current liabilities	£1,200 ▼
Non current liabilities	£3,700 ▼

BPP LEARNING MEDIA

Chapter 9

Task 9.1

	Duty	No duty
Before the auditor's report signed	✓	☐
After the auditor's report signed	☐	✓ After the auditor's report has been signed, the directors are responsible for drawing relevant subsequent events to the auditors' attention.

Task 9.2

Written representations are the written evidence of everything the directors have said to auditors during the audit.	False ▼ – it is written copy of certain required representations.
Auditors are required to get written confirmation from the directors of their responsibilities with regard to the financial statements.	True ▼

Task 9.3

The basic elements of the auditor's report

- A title, identifying to whom the audit report is addressed
- Addressee (normally the shareholders)
- An introductory paragraph, indicating the financial statements being audited
- A statement of management's responsibility for the financial statements
- A statement of the auditor's responsibility
- Opinions
- Auditor's address and signature of the auditors
- Date of the signature

Task 9.4

The directors refuse to write off a debt owed by Sandicore Ltd, a company that has gone into liquidation.	Qualified ▼ – this is restricted to receivables.
The auditors believe that the company is experiencing going concern issues. The directors have failed to disclose in the financial statements, claiming their recovery plan is going to get the company back on track. The auditors agree that the recovery plan has a high chance of success.	Qualified ▼ – this is a disagreement over going concern disclosures being omitted.

Task 9.5

The four possible types of opinion where there are matters that affect the auditor's opinion are:

(a) **Qualified opinion: inability to obtain sufficient appropriate audit evidence**

This qualified opinion is given where there has been an inability to obtain sufficient appropriate audit evidence in the auditors' work in one area. It is not considered to be pervasive but the auditor cannot give an opinion on it.

(b) **Disclaimer of opinion**

This opinion is given where the limitations on the scope of the auditors' work are so great that they cannot give an opinion on the truth and fairness of the financial statements.

(c) **Qualified opinion: financial statements are materially misstatement (except for)**

This qualified opinion is given where the auditors disagree with the treatment or disclosure of one item in the accounts which is considered material but not pervasive.

(d) **Adverse opinion**

This opinion is given where the auditors disagree with the treatment or disclosures in the financial statements so much that they do not believe that the financial statements give a true and fair view.

Task 9.6

Identify whether the financial statements appear to make sense.	Make sense ▾

Task 9.7

Going concern

(1) BCS

- Enquire whether the audit has been completed and what the results were
- Review any correspondence between BCS and Glad Rags
- If BCS require Glad Rags to undertake certain matters, discuss with Gladys and consider whether Glad Rags is able to make the changes
- Review the sales order book for the forthcoming period to assess whether BCS has withdrawn trade

(2) Potential sale of business

- Discuss with Gladys her plans, in particular the timescale of those plans
- Enquire if she intends to sell the business as a going concern and the likelihood of her being able to. Review any correspondence she has had with solicitors and or valuers/estate agents
- Review budgets for the forthcoming year for Glad Rags Limited to ensure that the company appears to still be operating as a going concern
- Discuss with Gladys whether she has implemented succession plans within the business, given that she is a key member of staff and integral to the business

Note: based on the information available at the time this book was written, we anticipate a task like this would be human marked in the real assessment.

....

Task 9.8

Opinion

In our opinion the financial statements:

- Give a true and fair view of the state of the company's affairs at 30 April 20X4 and of its profit for the year then ended; and
- Have been properly prepared, in accordance with United Kingdom Generally Accepted Accounting Practice; and
- Have been prepared in accordance with the Companies Act 2006;

Opinion on other matter prescribed by Companies Act 2006

- The information given in the Directors' Report is consistent with the financial statements.

....

Task 9.9

Identify whether the error requires to be adjusted or not adjusted to issue an unmodified audit opinion on the financial statements by selecting the appropriate option.	Needs to be adjusted ▼ The problem causing the inventory to be obsolete existed at the year end and therefore the inventory should be considered to be obsolete at the year end, even if it appeared to be saleable at the count.

Task 9.10

The auditors did not observe Handyco's inventory count at the year end, as they were not appointed until after that date. Due to the nature of the company's records, they have not been able to ascertain the existence of inventory by another method.	Modified ▼ – limitation on scope.
The auditors did not observe Complicateco's inventory count due to staffing difficulties on the day. The company has detailed inventory records, and the auditors were able to attend the premises two days later and carry out test counts against the company's records. The company had maintained a record of inventory existing on the year end date and movements since are easy to trace through the system.	Not modified ▼ – alternative procedures available.

Chapter 10

Task 10.1

The company being audited	Duty of care is automatic ▼
Individual shareholders in the company being audited	Duty of care must be proved ▼
The bank of the company being audited, who has given the company a substantial overdraft facility	Duty of care must be proved ▼

Task 10.2

A contract stating the maximum sum an auditor is liable for, or the maximum proportion of liability an auditor will accept responsibility for.	Liability limitation agreement ▼
A legal entity which bears some similarity to a company and gives similar legal protection to members in respect of liability.	Limited liability partnership ▼
Payments made to a third party to ensure a pay out to injured parties in the event of a negligence claim being successful.	Professional indemnity insurance ▼

Task 10.3

Working papers

Working papers are the documents on which auditors record their audit work. They may be paper format or on a computer.

Working papers must contain certain details. For example, they must state the name of the client, the year end being worked on, the name of the auditor doing the work and the date the work was done. They should also state the audit area, and contain the work done, the evidence obtained and conclusions drawn.

Confidentiality

The auditor has a duty to keep company affairs private. The auditor is likely to come across sensitive information when carrying out his audit and must not use that information to the advantage of a third party or to his own advantage.

Information about owner's intentions

In respect of the information concerning the director's intentions to sell the business, this information will impact on certain aspects of the audit work to be undertaken. However, the auditors have a duty not to mention this to other members of staff at Dowhop and to be circumspect with the information when attending the client – for example, not leaving working papers making reference to it lying around and even being discreet if wanting to talk to the director about it.

Task 10.4

The appropriate action is…	Decline the director's offer ▼

Being able to jump a three-year waiting list for a football season ticket is likely to be viewed as a big favour which could compromise your independence. Even if you are not of the mind to give in to client pressure, the client may feel in a position to exert pressure.

Sharing an executive box with the directors on a regular basis may entail receiving a certain amount of hospitality. It may also give the wrong impression to the world in general.

Task 10.5

Auditors' liability depends on whether negligent accountants owed a duty of care to those who have relied on their accounts. If the auditors knew a third party would rely and they failed to disclaim liability, they could be found liable.

(a) **The possibility of demonstrating negligence**

All APB pronouncements and in particular auditing standards are likely to be taken into account when the adequacy of the work of auditors is being considered in a court of law or in other contested situations.

In the case of Leesmoor Ltd, the auditors did not attend to observe the company's physical inventory count procedures, which is an accepted audit practice. Whether this was negligent would depend on whether or not the auditors could satisfy the court as to whether there were good practical reasons for non-attendance and the other audit work which they carried out in relation to inventory provided sufficient appropriate audit evidence on which to base their opinion. However, this may prove to be difficult.

(b) **The fact that the inventory figure in the financial statements apparently 'made sense'**

This suggests that the main audit evidence on which the auditors based their opinion, in relation to the inventory figure, was the result of their analytical procedures in this area. As the auditors seem, through pressure of work, to have neglected to attend the inventory count, then one would expect them to have carried out more extensive analytical procedures than would perhaps normally have been the case for that client. If it appeared that the auditors had only carried out a minimal amount of procedures, then they would very likely be open to a charge of negligence.

(c) **The fact that the auditors were not informed that the financial statements were to be used to obtain additional finance**

Past case law shows that judges do not care to attribute a duty of care to unknown third parties. It is unlikely that a judge would rule that the auditors had a duty of care to the lenders that they were unaware of, as there is no possibility that such a duty could have been implied in dealings between them.

....

Task 10.6

Report the matter to the firm's Money Laundering Reporting Officer ☑

This is a money laundering offence in the UK, despite where the bribery of government officials took place.

....

Task 10.7

The statement by the financial controller that assets had all been correctly valued is

| not likely to be reliable. | ▼ |

Answer bank

AAT AQ2013 SAMPLE ASSESSMENT
EXTERNAL AUDITING

Time allowed: 2 hours

Task 1

The external auditor may adopt an audit approach which involves undertaking either tests of control and substantive procedures or substantive procedures only, with no tests of controls.

For each of the following circumstances, identify the most likely approach to be adopted by the external auditor by selecting the appropriate option.

Circumstance	Tests of control and substantive procedures	Substantive procedures only, with no tests of control
The audited entity introduced a new integrated accounting software package at the beginning of the accounting period and is experiencing operational difficulties with it.	☐	☐
The audited entity undertakes a few transactions, each of which is individually material.	☐	☐
The audited entity has an internal audit function which routinely monitors operational and financial controls.	☐	☐

Task 2

Accounting systems have control objectives and control procedures to mitigate the risk that the control objective is not met.

Identify whether each of the following is a control objective, risk, or control procedure in respect of a purchases system by selecting the appropriate option.

(a) Purchasing unnecessary goods

[▼]

(b) Efficient use of working capital

[▼]

(c) Independent authorisation of purchase orders by purchasing manager

[▼]

Picklist:

Control objective
Risk
Control procedure

Task 3

Complete each of the following sentences, relating to internal control, by selecting the appropriate option.

(a) One of the objectives of an entity's internal control system is to provide reasonable assurance that the entity is [▼   ]

Picklist:

operating effectively and efficiently.
maximising shareholder wealth.

(b) The placing of restrictions on, and the requirement for the documentation of, employee activities so as to reduce the occurrence of errors and deviations are known as [▼   ]

Picklist:

detective controls.
preventative controls.

(c) The system for identifying potential events which could result in a failure to achieve business objectives and deciding on actions to address those potential events is known as the entity's [▼   ]

Picklist:

control environment.
risk assessment process.

Task 4

There are two types of assurance engagement which a practitioner is permitted to perform – a reasonable assurance engagement and a limited assurance engagement.

Identify whether the following statement, in respect of an external audit, is true or false by selecting the appropriate option.

An external audit conducted under International Standards on Auditing is a reasonable assurance engagement.

[▼   ]

Picklist:

True
False

Task 5

The external auditor of Mezzo Ltd has used an internal control questionnaire to assist him in his evaluation of internal controls over the revenue cycle.

Identify, for each of the following questions and answers, whether the answer indicates a control or a lack of control, by selecting the appropriate option.

(a) Are orders only accepted if there is sufficient inventory to fulfil the order? **YES**

▼

(b) Are customers required to sign a copy of the despatch note when they take delivery of goods? **NO**

▼

(c) Does the Sales Ledger Clerk perform a monthly reconciliation between the list of sales ledger balances and the balance on the sales ledger control account? **NO**

▼

Picklist:

Control
Lack of control

Task 6

The external auditor assesses control risk in order to determine the audit approach.

Identify, for each of the following factors, whether the auditor is likely to assess the control risk as being higher or lower, by selecting the appropriate option.

Factor	Higher	Lower
The audited entity has a process in place for reviewing the effectiveness of the entity's internal controls	☐	☐
The audited entity has recently brought payroll processing back in-house after a period of outsourcing	☐	☐
The audited entity has a policy of separating the functions of authorising and recording a transaction	☐	☐

Task 7

An entity uses internal control procedures to mitigate the risks to which it is exposed.

Listed below are two internal control procedures which are applicable to an entity's purchases system.

Match each risk mitigated to the internal control procedure by completing the table with the appropriate risk for the procedure.

Internal control procedure	Risk mitigated
The inventory system automatically generates purchase requisitions once an item of inventory reaches its minimum reorder level.	
Exception reporting of goods received records which do not have a corresponding invoice.	

Risks:

Unrecorded liabilities

Stockouts (running out of inventory)

Paying for goods not received

Task 8

The following are descriptions of procedures within the inventory system of Troll Ltd.

Identify whether each of the following procedures is a strength or a weakness by selecting the appropriate option.

(a) The warehouse manager, who is responsible for the day-to-day custody of the inventory, is also responsible for the year-end inventory count.

[▼]

(b) Staff are instructed to keep the movement of inventory during the year-end physical count to a minimum.

[▼]

Picklist:

Strength
Weakness

Task 9

The external auditor is required to undertake analytical procedures as part of the planning process to identify movements out of line with expectation.

The trade payables payment period of Bridge Ltd for the year ended 31 December 20X2 is 29 days compared to 36 days for the year ended 31 December 20X1.

Which TWO of the following may provide a plausible explanation for the fall in Bridge Ltd's trade payables payment period?

Suppliers' invoices relating to goods received in December 20X2
were posted to the ledger accounts in January 20X3 ☐

Suppliers' invoices relating to goods received in January 20X3
were posted to the ledger accounts in December 20X2 ☐

Suppliers have extended the credit terms available to Bridge Ltd ☐

Suppliers have tightened the credit terms available to Bridge Ltd ☐

Task 10

(a) **Which TWO of the following will INCREASE a sample size for tests of controls by more than a negligible amount?**

An increase in the tolerable rate of deviation ☐

An increase in the expected rate of deviation ☐

An increase in the number of sampling units in the population ☐

An increase in the auditor's desired level of assurance that the tolerable
rate of deviation is not exceeded by the actual rate of deviation ☐

The objective of a substantive test will determine the population from which the sample for testing is selected.

(b) **Identify, for the following objective, the population from which the sample should be selected by selecting the appropriate option.**

Obtain evidence of the completeness of cash sales.

| ▼ |

Picklist:

Cash book
Till records

Task 11

External auditors use analytical procedures, tests of control and tests of detail to gather audit evidence.

Identify whether each of the following procedures is an analytical procedure, a test of control or a test of detail by selecting the appropriate option.

(a) Comparing client data with similar prior period data.

▼

(b) Inspecting the work undertaken by the audited entity's internal audit function.

▼

(c) Vouching purchase invoices to goods received records.

▼

Picklist:

Analytical procedure
Test of control
Test of detail

Task 12

You are supervising the audit junior on the external audit of Waterford Ltd. The audit junior has been assigned the job of verifying the sales figure in the financial statements and you are responsible for devising procedures to test for OVERSTATEMENT of the sales figure.

Which TWO of the following procedures are the most suitable to test for overstatement of the sales figure?

Calculate the gross profit margin to ascertain whether it has increased compared to the previous year ☐

Calculate the gross profit margin to ascertain whether it has fallen compared to the previous year ☐

Trace pre year-end despatch records to pre year-end invoice entries in the sales account ☐

Vouch pre year-end invoice entries in the sales account to pre year-end despatch records ☐

Task 13

You are planning the external audit of Offaly Ltd for the year ended 31 December 20X1. The principal activity of Offaly Ltd is the manufacture of a range of electrical goods. On 19 December 20X1, the directors of Offaly Ltd announced a product recall of a recently launched product, which had been designed and developed by Offaly Ltd's research and development team. The product was recalled because, in a number of cases, the product had caught fire and resulted in personal injury. The product recall and injuries were both widely reported in the national press and on television.

Identify and explain the audit risks relating to the product recall. Your answer should refer to the specific items in the financial statements which may be at risk of misstatement.

Task 14

When testing transactions and balances, the external auditor will gain assurance about different assertions regarding those transactions and balances.

Identify, for each of the following assertions, the audit procedure that will provide assurance on it by completing the table with the audit procedure for the appropriate assertion.

Assertion	Audit procedure
Valuation	
Classification	
Cut-off	

The choices are:

Inspection of a supplier's invoice for the date of the transaction

Inspection of terms and conditions within a lease agreement

Tracing physical assets to entries in the accounting records

Inspection of impairment reviews undertaken by the audited entity's management

Task 15

Identify whether each of the following statements, in respect of computer-assisted audit techniques (CAATs), is true or false by selecting the appropriate option.

Statement	True	False
An integrated test facility involves introducing a fictitious entity into the audited entity's computer system and the running of test transactions on the records relating to the fictitious entity.	☐	☐
An advantage of the use of CAATs by an external auditor is that it permits the examination of large volumes of information stored on an audited entity's computer files at great speed.	☐	☐
The comparison of data on personnel and payroll master files to verify consistency is an example of how an external auditor may use test data.	☐	☐

Task 16

The external auditor is required to plan and perform an audit with professional scepticism, recognising that circumstances may exist that could cause the financial statements to be materially misstated.

Identify whether each of the following factors would be likely to cause the auditor to exercise a greater or a lesser degree of professional scepticism by selecting the appropriate option.

Factor	Greater professional scepticism	Lesser professional scepticism
The audited entity's management is unwilling to facilitate auditor access to key electronic files for testing through the use of computer assisted audit techniques (CAATs).	☐	☐
The audited entity's management is keen to implement recommendations made by internal and external auditors.	☐	☐

Task 17

The internal control checklist for Brandco Ltd indicates that procedures are in place to track the expiry dates of perishable inventory.

Identify whether or not this would provide assurance on each of the following control objectives by selecting the appropriate option.

Control objective	Assurance provided	No assurance provided
Cut off procedures are correctly applied	☐	☐
Obsolete inventory is minimised	☐	☐

Task 18

Audit documentation serves a number of purposes.

Identify the purpose of each of the following working papers by matching each reason for preparation to the appropriate working paper.

Working paper	Reason for preparation
Assessment of control risk	
Performance materiality calculations	
Details of how the engagement partner's review points have been cleared	

The choices are:

Determines the nature, timing and extent of audit procedures

Discharges quality control responsibilities

Determines the extent of reliance on internal controls

Task 19

Following the completion of audit testing in the external audit of Kildare Ltd, the total of unadjusted errors amounts to £20,000. The materiality threshold established by reference to key figures in the financial statements has been set at £50,000. If the financial statements were amended for these errors the profit figure will fall below the level that has to be achieved in order for the directors, who are minority shareholders, to earn their bonuses.

Identify whether or not the profit figure should be amended for the unadjusted errors so that an unmodified opinion on the financial statements can be issued by selecting the appropriate option.

▼

Picklist:

Amended
Not amended

Task 20

Athenry Ltd does not maintain continuous inventory records and consequently undertakes a full inventory count at its year end. The finance director of Athenry Ltd has informed the external auditor that the company intends to hold the inventory count on 27 June, three days before the 30 June year end.

The finance director will issue sequentially numbered inventory count sheets to the staff responsible for the count. These staff will record the quantity for each item of inventory and the finance director will calculate the year-end quantities of inventory by adjusting the inventory quantities at 27 June for movements in inventory between the count and the year end. To do this, he will add the quantities of goods received and deduct the quantities of goods despatched between the count and the year end. These movements will be obtained from the company's sequentially numbered goods received and despatch records.

Set out, in a manner suitable for inclusion in the audit plan, the audit procedures to be undertaken to ensure that the quantity of inventory is correctly reflected at 30 June.

Task 21

During the external audit of Gauguin Ltd, an interior design company, the audit junior has identified four purchase invoices which he considers to be unusual.

Which TWO of these purchase invoices should the audit junior definitely refer to his supervisor?

A purchase invoice for an individually material amount, posted to purchases ☐

A purchase invoice from the company's major shareholder,
for an insignificant amount, at a price double that paid to other suppliers ☐

An individually material invoice for the purchase of
decorating equipment, posted to property, plant and equipment ☐

An individually material invoice for the payment of consultancy fees,
posted to property, plant and equipment ☐

Task 22

During the external audit of Mayo Ltd, the audit junior discovered that staff in the buying department were buying goods from Kerry Ltd, a supplier which was not on Mayo Ltd's list of approved suppliers. The staff in the buying department informed the audit junior that they bought goods from Kerry Ltd because they were cheaper.

Identify which of the following courses of action the audit junior should take by selecting the appropriate option:

[▼]

Picklist:

No further action
Refer to supervisor

Task 23

Bantry Ltd has 50 employees who are all salaried and paid monthly. The payroll is processed by the payroll clerk, Nina, using an off-the-shelf software package. Nina is also responsible for maintaining the standing data and authorising and initiating the payment of salaries, which are transferred, electronically, into employees' bank accounts. The finance director notifies Nina, in writing, of standing data amendments, but does not have any other involvement in payroll processing.

Prepare extracts, suitable for inclusion in a report to the management of Bantry Ltd, which set out:

(i)   The possible consequences; and
(ii) The recommendations you would make

in respect of this matter.

Task 24

ISA 265 *Communicating deficiencies in internal control* defines a significant deficiency in internal control as a deficiency or combination of deficiencies in internal control that, in the auditors professional judgement, is of sufficient importance to merit the attention of those charged with governance.

Identify whether or not the following deficiency in internal control is a significant deficiency by selecting the appropriate option:

The identification of a fraud, relating to an immaterial monetary amount, carried out by management of the audited entity, which was not prevented by the entity's internal control system.

```
[                    ▼ ]
```

Picklist:

Not a significant deficiency
Significant deficiency

Task 25

Identify, for each of the following situations which have arisen at two unrelated audit clients, the type of audit opinion on the financial statements that should be expressed by selecting the appropriate option:

(a) During the current reporting period, the tax authorities commenced a major enquiry into all aspects of the tax affairs of Ebony Ltd. Until the enquiry is completed, it is not possible to estimate, with any reasonable degree of certainty, any ultimate liability which may fall upon the company. Consequently, no liability has been included in the financial statements. The directors have included a note, explaining the situation, in the financial statements. The engagement partner is satisfied that the note includes all the necessary disclosures for users of the financial statements to understand the situation.

```
[                    ▼ ]
```

Picklist:

Modified opinion
Unmodified opinion

(b) Ivory Ltd has included costs relating to the development of software used in its business in its statement of financial position. These costs include £250,000 of own labour capitalised, which is material to the financial statements. The amount is based on the finance director's estimate of time spent by employees on the development work. There are no time-sheets to support this estimate and there are no satisfactory audit procedures to confirm that labour costs have been appropriately capitalised.

▼

Picklist:

Qualified opinion due to material misstatement

Qualified opinion due to limitation on scope

Task 26

Norfolk LLP has resigned as external auditor of Fulford Ltd and is to be replaced by York LLP. York LLP wishes to communicate with Norfolk LLP to ascertain whether there is any professional reason why it should not accept appointment as external auditor of Fulford Ltd.

Which ONE of the following is the most appropriate action to be taken?

Norfolk LLP must obtain permission from Fulford Ltd to discuss its affairs with York LLP, but York LLP need not obtain permission from Fulford Ltd ☐

York LLP must obtain permission from Fulford Ltd to discuss its affairs with Norfolk LLP, but Norfolk LLP need not obtain permission from Fulford Ltd ☐

Both Norfolk LLP and York LLP must obtain permission from Fulford Ltd to discuss its affairs ☐

Task 27

Identify whether each of the following statements reflects an objective of an external audit of financial statements conducted under International Standards on Auditing (ISAs) by selecting the appropriate option.

Statement	Objective of an external audit	Not an objective of an external audit
Express an opinion on the future viability of the audited entity.	☐	☐
Express an opinion on whether the management of the audited entity has conducted the entity's affairs efficiently and effectively.	☐	☐
Express an opinion on whether the financial statements are prepared in accordance with an applicable financial reporting framework.	☐	☐

Task 28

Which ONE of the following best describes the parties to whom the external auditor may be liable if the external auditor is found guilty of professional negligence?

The shareholders of the audited entity and no other party ☐

The shareholders of the audited entity and third parties to whom a duty of care is established ☐

All parties who have relied on the external auditor's report in making an investment decision ☐

Task 29

Complete the following statement in respect of the role of the International Auditing and Assurance Standards Board (IAASB) by selecting the appropriate option.

The IAASB is responsible for setting auditing standards which

▼

Picklist:

Are compulsory around the world.
Facilitate the convergence of national and international standards.

Task 30

When inherent and control risk are assessed as high, the external auditor should reduce detection risk to keep audit risk at an acceptably low level.

Identity whether or not each of the following changes will reduce detection risk by selecting the appropriate option.

Change	Reduce	Not reduce
A lower materiality threshold when planning the audit	☐	☐
A lower level of professional scepticism	☐	☐
Performing substantive procedures on opening balances when a new external auditor has been appointed	☐	☐

Task 31

Complete the following statements relating to materiality by selecting the appropriate option.

(a) When determining percentages to be applied to figures in the financial statements to establish materiality thresholds, the percentage to be applied to profit before tax will

normally be [　　　　　　　　▼] than the percentage applied to total revenue.

(b) A misstatement which is confined to specific elements, accounts or items of the

financial statements would be considered [　　　　　　　▼]

Picklist:

(a) Higher / lower
(b) Material and pervasive. / material but not pervasive.

Task 32

Interview and listening skills are important tools for an external auditor in applying professional scepticism when interviewing a client.

In a meeting with the audit partner, the financial controller of Veritas Ltd started to mention to the audit partner that he was concerned that not all year-end inventories had been valued at the lower of cost and net realisable value. However, at that point, the finance director entered the room and the financial controller stated that in his opinion inventories had all been correctly valued.

Complete the following statement in respect of the reliability of the information provided by the financial controller by selecting the appropriate option.

The statement by the financial controller that inventories had all been correctly valued is

▼

Picklist:

Likely to be reliable.
Not likely to be reliable.

AAT AQ2013 SAMPLE ASSESSMENT EXTERNAL AUDITING

ANSWERS

Task 1

For each of the following circumstances, identify the most likely approach to be adopted by the external auditor by selecting the appropriate option.

Circumstance	Tests of control and substantive procedures	Substantive procedures only, with no tests of control
The audited entity introduced a new integrated accounting software package at the beginning of the accounting period and is experiencing operational difficulties with it.	☐	✓
The audited entity undertakes a few transactions, each of which is individually material.	☐	✓
The audited entity has an internal audit function which routinely monitors operational and financial controls.	✓	☐

Task 2

Identify whether each of the following is a control objective, risk, or control procedure in respect of a purchases system by selecting the appropriate option.

(a) Purchasing unnecessary goods

Risk	▼

(b) Efficient use of working capital

Control objective	▼

(c) Independent authorisation of purchase orders by purchasing manager

Control procedure	▼

Task 3

Complete each of the following sentences, relating to internal control, by selecting the appropriate option.

(a) One of the objectives of an entity's internal control system is to provide reasonable assurance that the entity is | operating effectively and efficiently. ▼ |

(b) The placing of restrictions on, and the requirement for the documentation of, employee activities so as to reduce the occurrence of errors and deviations are known as | preventive controls. ▼ |

(c) The system for identifying potential events which could result in a failure to achieve business objectives and deciding on actions to address those potential events is known as the entity's | risk assessment process. ▼ |

··

Task 4

There are two types of assurance engagement which a practitioner is permitted to perform – a reasonable assurance engagement and a limited assurance engagement.

Identify whether the following statement, in respect of an external audit, is true or false by selecting the appropriate option.

An external audit conducted under International Standards on Auditing is a reasonable assurance engagement.

| True ▼ |

··

Task 5

The external auditor of Mezzo Ltd has used an internal control questionnaire to assist him in his evaluation of internal controls over the revenue cycle.

Identify, for each of the following questions and answers, whether the answer indicates a control or a lack of control, by selecting the appropriate option.

(a) Are orders only accepted if there is sufficient inventory to fulfil the order? **YES**

Control ▼

(b) Are customers required to sign a copy of the despatch note when they take delivery of goods? **NO**

Lack of control ▼

(c) Does the Sales Ledger Clerk perform a monthly reconciliation between the list of sales ledger balances and the balance on the sales ledger control account? **NO**

Lack of control ▼

Task 6

Identify, for each of the following factors, whether the auditor is likely to assess the control risk as being higher or lower, by selecting the appropriate option.

Factor	Higher	Lower
The audited entity has a process in place for reviewing the effectiveness of the entity's internal controls		✓
The audited entity has recently brought payroll processing back in-house after a period of outsourcing	✓	
The audited entity has a policy of separating the functions of authorising and recording a transaction		✓

Task 7

Match each risk mitigated to the internal control procedure by completing the table with the appropriate risk for the procedure.

Internal control procedure	Risk mitigated
The inventory system automatically generates purchase requisitions once an item of inventory reaches its minimum reorder level.	Stockouts (running out of inventory)
Exception reporting of goods received records which do not have a corresponding invoice.	Unrecorded liabilities

Task 8

Identify whether each of the following procedures is a strength or a weakness by selecting the appropriate option.

(a) The warehouse manager, who is responsible for the day-to-day custody of the inventory, is also responsible for the year-end inventory count.

Weakness ▼

(b) Staff are instructed to keep the movement of inventory during the year-end physical count to a minimum.

Strength ▼

Task 9

Which TWO of the following may provide a plausible explanation for the fall in Bridge Ltd's trade payables payment period?

Suppliers' invoices relating to goods received in December 20X2 were posted to the ledger accounts in January 20X3 ☑

Suppliers' invoices relating to goods received in January 20X3 were posted to the ledger accounts in December 20X2 ☐

Suppliers have extended the credit terms available to Bridge Ltd ☐

Suppliers have tightened the credit terms available to Bridge Ltd ☑

Task 10

(a) **Which TWO of the following will INCREASE a sample size for tests of controls by more than a negligible amount?**

An increase in the tolerable rate of deviation ☐

An increase in the expected rate of deviation ☑

An increase in the number of sampling units in the population ☐

An increase in the auditor's desired level of assurance that the tolerable rate of deviation is not exceeded by the actual rate of deviation ☑

The objective of a substantive test will determine the population from which the sample for testing is selected.

(b) **Identify, for the following objective, the population from which the sample should be selected by selecting the appropriate option.**

Obtain evidence of the completeness of cash sales.

Till records ▼

Task 11

Identify whether each of the following procedures is an analytical procedure, a test of control or a test of detail by selecting the appropriate option.

(a) Comparing client data with similar prior period data.

Analytical procedure ▼

(b) Inspecting the work undertaken by the audited entity's internal audit function.

Test of control ▼

(c) Vouching purchase invoices to goods received records.

Test of detail ▼

Task 12

Which TWO of the following procedures are the most suitable to test for overstatement of the sales figure?

Calculate the gross profit margin to ascertain whether it has increased compared to the previous year ☑

Calculate the gross profit margin to ascertain whether it has fallen compared to the previous year ☐

Trace pre year-end despatch records to pre year-end invoice entries in the sales account ☐

Vouch pre year-end invoice entries in the sales account to pre year-end despatch records ☑

Task 13

Note: based on the information available at the time this book was written, we anticipate a task like this would be human marked in the real assessment.

Audit risks

Returns will require provisions for refunds to customers and increased provisions for warranties

These are estimates and as such prone to misstatement/May not be provided

Unsold inventory may now be worthless and will be overstated if not written down

Any development costs included in intangible assets may be impaired and will be overstated if impairment not reflected

Personal injury may fail rise to legal claims for damages which may require

- Provisions if expected outcome is probable
- Disclosure of contingent liabilities if expected outcome only possible

The company may fail to provide/disclose by the way of note

Adverse publicity may impact on going concern

- If uncertain this may not be disclosed in the notes to financial statements

- If the company has to cease trading, financial statements may not be prepared on the appropriate basis (i.e. break-up basis).

Task 14

Identify, for each of the following assertions, the audit procedure that will provide assurance on it by completing the table with the audit procedure for the appropriate assertion.

Assertion	Audit procedure
Valuation	Inspection of impairment reviews undertaken by the audited entity's management
Classification	Inspection of terms and conditions within a lease agreement
Cut-off	Inspection of a supplier's invoice for the date of the transaction

Task 15

Identify whether each of the following statements, in respect of computer-assisted audit techniques (CAATs), is true or false by selecting the appropriate option.

Statement	True	False
An integrated test facility involves introducing a fictitious entity into the audited entity's computer system and the running of test transactions on the records relating to the fictitious entity.	✓	
An advantage of the use of CAATs by an external auditor is that it permits the examination of large volumes of information stored on an audited entity's computer files at great speed.	✓	
The comparison of data on personnel and payroll master files to verify consistency is an example of how an external auditor may use test data.		✓

Task 16

Identify whether each of the following factors would be likely to cause the auditor to exercise a greater or a lesser degree of professional scepticism by selecting the appropriate option.

Factor	Greater professional scepticism	Lesser professional scepticism
The audited entity's management is unwilling to facilitate auditor access to key electronic files for testing through the use of computer assisted audit techniques (CAATs).	✓	
The audited entity's management is keen to implement recommendations made by internal and external auditors.		✓

Task 17

Identify whether or not this would provide assurance on each of the following control objectives by selecting the appropriate option.

Control objective	Assurance provided	No assurance provided
Cut off procedures are correctly applied	☐	✓
Obsolete inventory is minimised	✓	☐

Task 18

Identify the purpose of each of the following working papers by matching each reason for preparation to the appropriate working paper.

Working paper	Reason for preparation
Assessment of control risk	Determines the extent of reliance on internal controls
Performance materiality calculations	Determines the nature, timing and extent of audit procedures
Details of how the engagement partner's review points have been cleared	Discharges quality control responsibilities

Task 19

Following the completion of audit testing in the external audit of Kildare Ltd, the total of unadjusted errors amounts to £20,000. The materiality threshold established by reference to key figures in the financial statements has been set at £50,000. If the financial statements were amended for these errors the profit figure will fall below the level that has to be achieved in order for the directors, who are minority shareholders, to earn their bonuses.

Identify whether or not the profit figure should be amended for the unadjusted errors so that an unmodified opinion on the financial statements can be issued by selecting the appropriate option.

Amended ▼

Task 20

Note: based on the information available at the time this book was written, we anticipate a task like this would be human marked in the real assessment.

Attend inventory count on 27 June

Assess adequacy of procedures – counting in pairs, marking of items once counted, control over inventory movements etc

Check completeness of sequence of returned count sheet

Obtain numbers of last goods received and despatch records on 27 June and 30 June

Obtain FD's workings relating to inventory adjustments

Re-perform FD's calculations

Vouch movements in to goods received records between 27 and 30 June

Vouch movements out to despatch records between 27 and 30 June

Inspect goods returned records (in and out) between 27 and 30 June to ensure adjustment made

Ensure any inventory movements on 27 June are not double counted

---

Task 21

Which TWO of these purchase invoices should the audit junior definitely refer to his supervisor?

A purchase invoice for an individually material amount, posted to purchases ☐

A purchase invoice from the company's major shareholder,
for an insignificant amount, at a price double that paid to other suppliers ☑

An individually material invoice for the purchase of
decorating equipment, posted to property, plant and equipment ☐

An individually material invoice for the payment of consultancy fees,
posted to property, plant and equipment ☑

Task 22

Identify which of the following courses of action the audit junior should take by selecting the appropriate option:

Refer to supervisor ▼

Task 23

Note: based on the information available at the time this book was written, we anticipate a task like this would be human marked in the real assessment.

Consequences

Fraud and errors may occur and remain undetected

Nina could

- Make an error when setting up standing data
- Insert fictitious names on the payroll and divert funds into her own bank account
- Inflate salaries (her own and/or colleagues).

Recommendation

Segregation of duties between payroll preparation and maintenance of standing data authorisation and initiation of payment

Separate passwords for standing data amendment and initiation of payment

Payroll authorisation to be evidenced by signature on the payroll

All amendments to standing data to be checked to FD's notification

Standing data to be printed out periodically and checked to personnel records

---

Task 24

ISA 265 *Communicating deficiencies in internal control* defines a significant deficiency in internal control as a deficiency or combination of deficiencies in internal control that, in the auditors professional judgement, is of sufficient importance to merit the attention of those charged with governance.

Identify whether or not the following deficiency in internal control is a significant deficiency by selecting the appropriate option:

The identification of a fraud, relating to an immaterial monetary amount, carried out by management of the audited entity, which was not prevented by the entity's internal control system.

Significant deficiency ▼

Task 25

Identify, for each of the following situations which have arisen at two unrelated audit clients, the type of audit opinion on the financial statements that should be expressed by selecting the appropriate option:

(a) During the current reporting period, the tax authorities commenced a major enquiry into all aspects of the tax affairs of Ebony Ltd. Until the enquiry is completed, it is not possible to estimate, with any reasonable degree of certainty, any ultimate liability which may fall upon the company. Consequently, no liability has been included in the financial statements. The directors have included a note, explaining the situation, in the financial statements. The engagement partner is satisfied that the note includes all the necessary disclosures for users of the financial statements to understand the situation.

> Unmodified opinion ▼

(b) Ivory Ltd has included costs relating to the development of software used in its business in its statement of financial position. These costs include £250,000 of own labour capitalised, which is material to the financial statements. The amount is based on the finance director's estimate of time spent by employees on the development work. There are no time-sheets to support this estimate and there are no satisfactory audit procedures to confirm that labour costs have been appropriately capitalised.

> Qualified opinion due to limitation on scope ▼

Task 26

Which ONE of the following is the most appropriate action to be taken?

Norfolk LLP must obtain permission from Fulford Ltd to discuss its affairs with York LLP, but York LLP need not obtain permission from Fulford Ltd ☐

York LLP must obtain permission from Fulford Ltd to discuss its affairs with Norfolk LLP, but Norfolk LLP need not obtain permission from Fulford Ltd ☐

Both Norfolk LLP and York LLP must obtain permission from Fulford Ltd to discuss its affairs ☑

Task 27

Identify whether each of the following statements reflects an objective of an external audit of financial statements conducted under International Standards on Auditing (ISAs) by selecting the appropriate option.

Statement	Objective of an external audit	Not an objective of an external audit
Express an opinion on the future viability of the audited entity.	☐	✓
Express an opinion on whether the management of the audited entity has conducted the entity's affairs efficiently and effectively.	☐	✓
Express an opinion on whether the financial statements are prepared in accordance with an applicable financial reporting framework.	✓	☐

Task 28

Which ONE of the following best describes the parties to whom the external auditor may be liable if the external auditor is found guilty of professional negligence?

The shareholders of the audited entity and no other party ☐

The shareholders of the audited entity and third parties to whom a duty of care is established ✓

All parties who have relied on the external auditor's report in making an investment decision ☐

Task 29

Complete the following statement in respect of the role of the International Auditing and Assurance Standards Board (IAASB) by selecting the appropriate option.

The IAASB is responsible for setting auditing standards which

facilitate the convergence of national and international standard ▼

Task 30

Identity whether or not each of the following changes will reduce detection risk by selecting the appropriate option.

Change	Reduce	Not reduce
A lower materiality threshold when planning the audit	✓	☐
A lower level of professional scepticism	☐	✓
Performing substantive procedures on opening balances when a new external auditor has been appointed	✓	☐

Task 31

Complete the following statements relating to materiality by selecting the appropriate option.

(a) When determining percentages to be applied to figures in the financial statements to establish materiality thresholds, the percentage to be applied to profit before tax will normally be | higher ▼ | than the percentage applied to total revenue.

(b) A misstatement which is confined to specific elements, accounts or items of the financial statements would be considered | material but not pervasive ▼ |

Task 32

Complete the following statement in respect of the reliability of the information provided by the financial controller by selecting the appropriate option.

The statement by the financial controller that inventories had all been correctly valued is

| not likely to be reliable ▼ |

BPP PRACTICE ASSESSMENT 1
EXTERNAL AUDITING

Time allowed: 2 hours

External auditing

Task 1

The external auditor may seek to place reliance on internal controls in order to restrict substantive testing.

For each of the following circumstances, identify whether the external auditor is likely to place reliance, or place no reliance on internal controls by selecting the appropriate option.

	Reliance	No reliance
New members of the accounting team are given a controls manual, and where possible, asked to shadow their predecessor to learn the relevant controls for their position.	☐	☐
Control activities are reviewed on an annual basis after the annual audit, and improvements made if seen fit.	☐	☐
No member of the accounts team has any formal accountancy training, and prior year files show that audit recommendations relating to controls are not implemented.	☐	☐

Task 2

Accounting systems have control objectives and control procedures to mitigate the risks that the control objective is not met.

Identify whether each of the following is a control objective, risk or control procedure by selecting the appropriate option.

Order forms are pre-numbered.	▼
Orders are only taken when current account balances have been checked.	▼
Orders may not be recorded.	▼

Picklist:

Control objective
Risk
Control procedure

Task 3

Complete the following definitions relating to internal controls, by selecting the appropriate option.

The control [_____ ▼] includes the governance and management functions, and the attitudes, awareness and actions of directors and management concerning the entity's internal control and its importance in the entity.

Control [_____ ▼] are policies and procedures established to achieve the entity's specific objectives.

[_____ ▼] of controls is a process to assess the quality of internal control performance over time.

Picklist:

Objectives
Environment
Activities
Actions
Monitoring
Planning

Task 4

The concept of assurance is important in auditing.

Identify whether the sentence below is a definition of reasonable or limited assurance, by selecting the appropriate option.

	Reasonable assurance	Limited assurance
A high, but not absolute, level of assurance.	☐	☐

Task 5

Creditco Ltd is a company which issues loans. It has few staff. It charges interest on a sliding scale, depending on the value and length of the loan.

Which THREE of the following items are likely to be subject to external audit?

Interest income ☐

Cash ☐

Payables ☐

Receivables ☐

Task 6

The external auditor assesses control risk in order to determine the audit approach.

Identify, for each of the following factors, whether it is likely to lead to the auditor assessing that there is an increase or a decrease in control risk, by selecting the appropriate option.

Factor	Increase or decrease in risk
The framework within which an entity's activities for achieving its objectives are planned, executed, controlled and reviewed.	▼
There is a large staff in the accounting department, and key areas are segregated between different staff.	▼
Financial statements are produced by the financial controller after he has carried out a large number of journals to get things in order.	▼

Picklist:

Increase
Decrease

Task 7

An entity uses internal control procedures in order to mitigate the risks to which the entity is exposed. Listed below are two internal control procedures which are applicable to an entity's non current asset procurement system.

Match each risk mitigated to the internal control procedure by completing the table with the appropriate risk to the procedures.

Internal control procedure	Risk mitigated
Monthly capital expenditure budget prepared.	
Capital expenditure purchase orders approved at monthly directors' meetings	

Picklist:

Assets purchased for personal use.

Assets paid for when not received.

Company does not have access to appropriate assets when required.

Company buys assets at the best price.

Task 8

The following are descriptions of procedures within the sales system of New Jersey Ltd.

For each procedure, identify whether it is a strength or a deficiency, by selecting the appropriate option.

Procedure	Strength or deficiency
Jane is in charge of invoice processing and Amelia is in charge of cash receipts.	▼
Amelia banks cash receipts once a week.	▼

Picklist:

Strength
Deficiency

Task 9

The external auditor is required to undertake analytical procedures as part of the planning process in order to identify the risk of misstatement of figures in the financial statements. The results of analytical procedures conducted on non-current assets are shown below.

Identify whether the results indicate that non-current assets might have been under or overstated, by selecting the appropriate option.

The results show that:	
Non current assets cost has increased by 5%, while the directors claim that there have been no additions to non current assets.	▼
The repairs and maintenance cost is usually about 3% of total non current assets. This year it was 25%.	▼

Picklist:

Understated
Overstated

··

Task 10

When selecting items to in order to perform tests of detail, the auditor has to consider a number of factors.

Identify, for each of the following factors, the impact they will have on sample size, by selecting the appropriate option.

Factor	Impact on sample size
Increase in tolerable misstatement.	▼
Increase in expected misstatement.	▼
Increase in number of sampling units.	▼

Picklist:

Increase
Decrease
No effect

··

Task 11

Auditors use tests of control and substantive procedures to gather audit evidence.

Identify, for each of the procedures below, whether it is a test of control or a substantive procedure by selecting the appropriate option.

	Test of control	Substantive procedure
Inspection of reconciliation between purchase ledger and supplier statement	☐	☐
Reconciliation of purchase ledger balance to supplier statement.	☐	☐
Comparison of year end payables balance with prior year payables balance.	☐	☐

Task 12

An audit junior performed a reconciliation of a sample of trade payables balances of Elm Ltd to supplier statements at 30 April 20X5. One balance has been reconciled as follows:

	£
Balance as per supplier statement	25,038
Invoice 30 April 20X5 – not on Elm's ledger	(583)
Credit requested 24 February 20X5 – damaged goods	(1,005)
Balance due per purchases ledger	23,450

The junior has asked for guidance on the further work to be performed in respect of this reconciliation.

Identify which piece of evidence each of the reconciling items should be checked to by matching the appropriate evidence with the reconciling item:

(i)   Invoice [   ]

(ii) Credit request [   ]

Picklist:

Goods returned note
Purchase invoice
Goods received note
Goods despatched note

Task 13

During the year ended 30 June 20X2, Carling Ltd entered an agreement with a customer, Beck, to allow Carling to store Carling's products at Beck's premises. Beck customers sells the goods to other parties. Carling only accounts for a sale to Beck when Beck has arranged a sale to a third party.

Set out, in a manner suitable for inclusion in the audit plan:

(i)   **The audit risks relating to inventory resulting from this agreement**

(ii) **The procedures to be taken to ensure that inventory is fairly stated in the financial statements**

Task 14

As part of verification techniques in respect of non current assets, an auditor is going to inspect hire purchase agreements. The auditor will gain assurance about different assertions depending on the information on the agreements.

In respect of the information below, select the assertion for which that information will provide primary assurance.

Information	Assertion	
Description of the agreement entered into		▼
Contract price		▼
Date of the agreement		▼

Picklist:

Existence
Completeness
Valuation
Rights and obligations

Task 15

Identify whether the following statements in respect of Computer Assisted Audit Techniques (CAATs) are true or false, by selecting the appropriate option.

	True	False
Auditors may use CAATs at will.	☐	☐
Auditors may use test data in which they process false data to ensure that the system rejects it.	☐	☐
Auditors may use test data to compare data on personnel and payroll master files to ensure consistency.	☐	☐

Task 16

An external auditor is required to obtain an understanding of the control environment within an audited entity.

Identify whether the following factors contribute to a strong control environment or a weak control environment or have no effect, by selecting the appropriate option.

A company's staff is competent and acts with integrity.	▼
The directors assess fraud and compliance risks on a monthly basis.	▼

Picklist:

Strong
Weak
No effect

Task 17

External auditors use a variety of methods for documenting systems of control, including flowcharts, internal control questionnaires and narrative notes.

Identify for each of the following situations, the method which seems most appropriate by selecting the relevant option.

It is a new client. The audit manager wants a comprehensive description of the complex system before it is evaluated.	▼
It is an existing client. The auditors have always relied on controls, but management has recently overhauled the controls system in an attempt to make cost savings. The audit manager is keen to ensure that the new system is capable of mitigating control risk.	▼

Picklist:

Narrative notes
Flowchart
Internal control questionnaire

Task 18

Identify whether the following statements in respect of an external auditor's working papers are true or false by selecting the appropriate option.

Auditors are not legally required to maintain working papers.	▼
Working papers give evidence of whether audit work was carried out in line with auditing standards.	▼
Working papers should be labelled with who prepared and who reviewed the working paper, and when those actions were carried out.	▼

Picklist:

True
False

Task 19

During the audit of Cancer Ltd, when carrying out a purchases cut off test, the auditors discovered that a batch of goods received in the last few days of the year have been processed in the purchases ledger for the following year. Inventory is not part of the accounting records of Cancer. Inventory on the premises at the year end is counted, and added into the financial statements by journal entry.

Select the effect that this has on the financial statements at the year end.

Inventory		▼
Purchases		▼
Payables		▼

Picklist:

Overstated
Understated
No effect

Task 20

You are planning the audit of receivables at Girlco Ltd. Girlco is an established client, and you attended the previous audit. Girlco has a large sales ledger and there is a high sample size for the audit of receivables. In previous years, customers have not been circularised and the client has requested that you do not circularise customers. Receivables is considered to be low risk, as customers usually pay promptly. This year, Girlco has had a long running dispute with one customer, Ravenna Ltd, about the quality of goods supplied. Ravenna is threatening to find another supplier if the quality problems are not resolved soon.

Set out, in a manner suitable for inclusion in the audit plan, the audit procedures to be undertaken in order to ensure that the receivables balance is fairly stated in the financial statements.

Task 21

During the audit of Trout Ltd for the year ended 31 December 20X1, the audit junior identified three instances of sales receipts being posted to the wrong ledger account. The sample was extended, and the control fault found to be isolated. Discussion with client staff indicated all three errors occurred in one week in August, when the sales ledger clerk was on holiday. ·

In respect of this matter, select what action the audit junior should take.	▼

Picklist:

Refer to supervisor
Take no further action

Task 22

During the audit of HeartCo Ltd, the audit junior identified that the company had purchased a new car in the year which is for the sole use of the managing director's wife, who does not work in the business. The value of the car has been verified to invoice, and it is being depreciated in line with other company cars, over four years.

In respect of this matter, select what the audit junior should do next.	▼

Picklist:

No further action
Refer to supervisor

Task 23

During the audit of Smartco Ltd it was discovered that warehouse staff agree delivery documentation against a purchase order when items are delivered (if such delivery documentation exists), sign the document, one part of which is returned to the supplier and the other of which is filed with the purchase order in the warehouse office.

Prepare extracts, suitable for inclusion in a report to management of Smartco Ltd, which set out

(i) **The possible consequences, and**
(ii) **The recommendations that you would make**

in respect of this matter

Task 24

ISA 265 *Communicating deficiencies in internal control to those charged with governance and management* defines a significant deficiency in internal control as a deficiency or combination of deficiencies in internal control that, in the auditor's professional judgement, is of sufficient importance to merit the attention of those charged with governance.

Identify whether or not the following deficiency in internal control is a significant deficiency by selecting the appropriate option:

A sales invoice for £50 which has been misposted between customer accounts on the sales ledger.	▼

Picklist:

Significant
Not significant

Task 25

For each of the following situations which have arisen in two unrelated audit clients, select whether or not the audit opinion on the financial statements would be modified.

Materiality is assessed at 5% of profit before tax.

Helena Ltd has profit before tax of £140,000. The directors have included in trade receivables a debt of £6,000. The customer has recently gone into administration.	▼
There was a flood at Douglas Ltd and several sales invoice files were destroyed. A copy of the sales invoice is matched with the goods despatched form and kept in the unaffected warehouse stores for twelve months.	▼

Picklist:

Modified
Not modified

Task 26

During the audit of Gala Ltd, the audit senior discovered that the purchases director accepts bonuses from suppliers for using them. Discussion with personnel in the personal tax department revealed that these bonuses do not appear on the director's personal tax return.

Which ONE of the following is the appropriate action for the audit senior to take?

Report the matter to:

The board of directors ☐

The personal tax department of the firm ☐

HMRC ☐

The money laundering reporting officer of the firm ☐

Task 27

Complete the following statement on the UK legal requirements on a company to keep accounting records.

Every company must keep adequate accounting records. Adequate accounting records means records that are sufficient to:

(a) Show and explain the company's [▼]

(b) Disclose with reasonable accuracy, at any time, the [▼] of the company at that time, and

(c) Enable the [▼] to ensure that any accounts required to be prepared comply with the requirements of the Companies Act.

Picklist:

Directors
Transactions
Balances
Financial position
Disclosures
Financial statements

Task 28

Which ONE of the following best describes audit failure?

Audit resulting in the auditors being found guilty of negligence [ ]

Audit resulting in a modified audit opinion [ ]

Audit failing to uncover a fraud perpetrated by the managing director [ ]

Audit resulting in a qualified audit opinion [ ]

Task 29

Identify whether the following statement in respect of external auditors' professional standards is true or false.

UK auditors are required to follow the guidance of International Standards on Auditing (ISAs) issued by the Codes and Standards Committee of the Financial Reporting Council.	▼

Picklist:

True
False

....

Task 30

When planning an audit of financial statements, the external auditor is required to consider how factors such as the entity's operating environment and its system of internal control affect the risk of misstatement in the financial statements.

Identify whether the following factors are likely to increase or reduce the risk of misstatement or have no effect, by selecting the appropriate option.

Directors communicate and enforce integrity and ethical values.	▼
Top managers are offered profit related bonuses, which are scaled according to the level of profit achieved.	▼
The entity has not taken any action about matters raised in the report to management from the previous three audits.	▼

Picklist:

Increase
Reduce
No effect

....

Task 31

Identify whether the following statements in respect of materiality are true or false, by selecting the appropriate option.

A percentage guide for materiality is often used, for example 5% of profits.	▼
Performance materiality is the amount or amounts set by the auditor at more than materiality for the financial statements as a whole to reduce to an appropriately low level the probability that the aggregate of uncorrected and undetected misstatements exceeds materiality for the financial statements as a whole.	▼

Picklist:

True
False

Task 32

During the audit of FreshCo Ltd, the audit senior had a long conversation with the financial controller about how the material warranty provision had been calculated.

Identify whether or not the following statement concerning that conversation is true or false, by selecting the appropriate option.

The audit senior should document the conversation he has had with the financial controller about the warranty provision in notes on the audit file.	▼

Picklist:

True
False

BPP PRACTICE ASSESSMENT 1
EXTERNAL AUDITING

ANSWERS

External auditing

Task 1

	Reliance	No reliance
New members of the accounting team are given a controls manual, and where possible, asked to shadow their predecessor to learn the relevant controls for their position.	✓	☐
Control activities are reviewed on an annual basis after the annual audit, and improvements made if seen fit.	✓	☐
No member of the accounts team has any formal accountancy training, and prior year files show that audit recommendations relating to controls are not implemented.	☐	✓

Task 2

Order forms are pre-numbered.	Control procedure ▼
Orders are only taken when current account balances have been checked.	Control procedure ▼
Orders may not be recorded.	Risk ▼

Task 3

The control **environment** ▼ includes the governance and management functions, and the attitudes, awareness and actions of directors and management concerning the entity's internal control and its importance in the entity.

Control **activities** ▼ are policies and procedures established to achieve the entity's specific objectives.

Monitoring ▼ of controls is a process to assess the quality of internal control over time.

Task 4

	Reasonable assurance	Limited assurance
A high, but not absolute level of assurance.	✓	☐

Task 5

Interest income ✓

Cash ✓

Payables ☐

Receivables ✓

Task 6

Factor	Increase or decrease in risk
The framework within which an entity's activities for achieving its objectives are planned, executed, controlled and reviewed.	Decrease ▼
There is a large staff in the accounting department, and key areas are segregated between different staff.	Decrease ▼
Financial statements are produced by the financial controller after he has carried out a large number of journals to get things in order.	Increase ▼

Task 7

Internal control procedure	Risk mitigated
Monthly capital expenditure budget prepared.	Company does not have access to appropriate assets when required.
Capex purchase orders approved at monthly directors' meetings	Assets purchased for personal use.

Task 8

Procedure	Strength or deficiency
Jane is in charge of invoice processing and Amelia is in charge of cash receipts.	Strength – indicates segregation of duties ▼
Amelia banks cash receipts once a week.	Deficiency – cash should be banked more frequently if possible. ▼

Task 9

The results show that:	
Non current assets cost has increased by 5%, while the directors claim that there have been no additions to non current assets.	Overstated – **cost** can only increase by additions. ▼
The repairs and maintenance cost is usually about 3% of total non current assets. This year it was 25%.	Understated – a capital item may have been expensed in repairs and maintenance. ▼

Task 10

Factor	Impact on sample size
Increase in tolerable misstatement.	Decrease ▼
Increase in expected misstatement.	Increase ▼
Increase in number of sampling units.	No effect ▼

Task 11

	Test of control	Substantive procedure
Inspection of reconciliation between purchase ledger and supplier statement	✓	☐
Reconciliation of purchase ledger balance to supplier statement.	☐	✓
Comparison of year end payables balance with prior year payables balance.	☐	✓

Task 12

(i)   Invoice – goods received note (if goods were received in the year, invoice should be included)

(ii) Credit request – goods returned note (if goods have been returned, and credit pending is dealt with properly, okay to omit)

Task 13

(i)   Audit risks

- There is a risk that inventory will be wrongly excluded or included in the financial statements due to confusion over who owns the inventory at the critical time
- There is an increase in detection risk as the auditor now has another venue to consider when carrying out the inventory count

(ii) Procedures

- Review terms of the contract to understand the agreement between the parties
- Attend third party premises on day of inventory count and ascertain if inventory is suitably isolated and cut off procedures exist/operate adequately
- Confirm inventory held with third party in writing
- Perform cut off tests between sales by (and therefore to) the third party and inventory in count

Note: based on the information available at the time this book was written, we anticipate a task like this would be human marked in the real assessment.

Task 14

Information	Assertion	
Description of the agreement entered into	Rights and obligations	▼
Contract price	Valuation	▼
Date of the agreement	Completeness	▼

Task 15

	True	False
Auditors may use CAATs at will.	☐	☑ – they must have client permission.
Auditors may use test data in which they process false data to ensure that the system rejects it.	☑	☐
Auditors may use test data to compare data on personnel and payroll master files to ensure consistency.	☐	☑

Task 16

A company's staff is competent and acts with integrity.	No effect ▼ – control environment is to do with the actions, awareness and attitude of **management** and **those charged with governance**.	
The directors assess fraud and compliance risks on a monthly basis.	Strong ▼	

Task 17

It is a new client. The audit manager wants a comprehensive description of the complex system before it is evaluated.	Narrative notes ▼ – it is a complex system so flowchart inappropriate. An ICQ evaluates and records.
It is an existing client. The auditors have always relied on controls, but management has recently overhauled the controls system in an attempt to make cost savings. The audit manager is keen to ensure that the new system is capable of mitigating control risk.	Internal control questionnaire ▼

Task 18

Auditors are not legally required to maintain working papers.	True ▼
Working papers give evidence of whether audit work was carried out in line with auditing standards.	True ▼
Working papers should be labelled with who prepared and who reviewed the working paper, and when those actions were carried out.	True ▼

Task 19

Inventory	No effect ▼
Purchases	Understated ▼
Payables	Understated ▼

Task 20

* Obtain sales ledger print out showing sales receipts after the year end

* Vouch sales receipts after the year end for a sample of accounts to after date bank statements to ensure account balances are cleared systematically (ie oldest first)

* Perform analytical procedures on sales ledger balances compared to previous year (in particular focus on Ravenna balance)

* Scrutinise sales ledger for old balances (particularly on Ravenna balance)

* Discuss allowance for doubtful debts with credit controller and assess if appropriate

* Review correspondence with Ravenna to assess likelihood of any outstanding balance being paid

Note: based on the information available at the time this book was written, we anticipate a task like this would be human marked in the real assessment.

Task 21

In respect of this matter, select what action the audit junior should take.	Take no further action ▼

Task 22

In respect of this matter, select what the audit junior should do next.	Refer to supervisor. ▼

Task 23

(i) Consequences

- If delivery documentation is not provided by the supplier, it is possible no check is made on what the delivery is

- No check is made on whether the delivery matches the documentation

- No check is made on whether the goods are a suitable quality/state to be accepted by the business

- No link appears to be made between goods being received in the warehouse and invoices being received in the accounts department

(ii) Recommendations

- The items delivered should be checked to the delivery documentation and the order in terms of quantity and quality before the goods (and by implication, the liability in respect of them) are accepted and signed for

- Ideally, an internal goods received note (GRN) should be raised

- Any issues should be noted on the delivery documentation and a goods return note raised to return with the goods if items are not appropriate

- The purchase order and related delivery documentation (delivery note or GRN) or copy goods return note should be sent to the accounts department to be matched to the invoice

Note: based on the information available at the time this book was written, we anticipate a task like this would be human marked in the real assessment.

Task 24

A sales invoice for £50 which has been misposted between customer accounts on the sales ledger.	Not significant ▼

Task 25

Helena Ltd has profit before tax of £140,000. The directors have included in trade receivables a debt of £6,000. The customer has recently gone into administration.	Not modified	▼
There was a flood at Douglas Ltd and several sales invoice files were destroyed. A copy of the sales invoice is matched with the goods despatched form and kept in the unaffected warehouse stores for twelve months.	Not modified	▼

Task 26

The money laundering reporting officer of the firm ✓

Task 27

Every company must keep adequate accounting records. Adequate accounting records means records that are sufficient to:

(a) Show and explain the company's **transactions** ▼

(b) Disclose with reasonable accuracy, at any time, the **financial position** ▼ of the company at that time, and

(c) Enable the **directors** ▼ to ensure that any accounts required to be prepared comply with the requirements of the Companies Act.

Task 28

Audit resulting in the auditors being found guilty of negligence. ✓

Although auditors must plan and perform audits with an expectation of discovering fraud causing material misstatement, an MD is in a position to conceal fraudulent activity and an adequately performed audit might not uncover such a fraud. Modified and qualified audit opinions are legitimate outcomes of a quality audit.

Task 29

UK auditors are required to follow the guidance of International Standards on Auditing (ISAs) issued by the Codes and Standards Committee of the Financial Reporting Council	True ▼

Task 30

Directors communicate and enforce integrity and ethical values.	Reduce ▼
Top managers are offered profit related bonuses, which are scaled according to the level of profit achieved.	Increase ▼
The entity has not taken any action about matters raised in the report to management from the previous three audits.	Increase ▼

Task 31

A percentage guide for materiality is often used, for example 5% of profits.	True ▼
Performance materiality is the amount or amounts set by the auditor at more than materiality for the financial statements as a whole to reduce to an appropriately low level the probability that the aggregate of uncorrected and undetected misstatements exceeds materiality for the financial statements as a whole.	False ▼ – it is less than materiality

Task 32

The audit senior should document the conversation he has had with the financial controller about the warranty provision in notes on the audit file.	True ▼

BPP PRACTICE ASSESSMENT 2
EXTERNAL AUDITING

Time allowed: 2 hours

External auditing

Task 1

The external auditor may seek to place reliance on internal controls in order to restrict substantive testing.

Identify, in each of the following circumstances, whether the external auditor is likely or unlikely to place reliance on internal controls by selecting the appropriate option.

	Likely	Unlikely
Lizbet Ltd has been a client for two years. After the previous two audits, the firm raised control issues with the client in a report to management, and the recommendations were implemented. The directors are keen to improve the company's operations. The audit team has not relied on controls in the previous audits.	☐	☐
Mattieu Ltd is a new client. An audit team has ascertained its controls system, which is extensive, and have been given access to the internal audit department's most recent report on controls.	☐	☐
Emilie Ltd is an established client. The managing director is closely involved in all key aspects of the business and favours getting things done over following the book.	☐	☐

Task 2

Accounting systems have control objectives and control procedures to mitigate the risks that the control objective is not met.

For each of the following, select whether they are a control objective, risk or control procedure.

Company pays the correct employees	▾
Company pays the incorrect employees	▾
Company checks pay against budgets	▾

Picklist:

Control objective
Risk
Control procedure

Task 3

Which ONE of the following is NOT a limitation of internal control systems?

Human error in executing the controls ☐

Human error in designing the controls ☐

Collusion in circumventing the controls ☐

Lack of an internal audit function to monitor the controls ☐

Task 4

Which ONE of the following is a description of negative assurance?

A statement that nothing has come to the practitioner's attention to indicate that a true and fair view is not given ☐

A statement that the practitioner cannot tell whether a true and fair view is given due to insufficient evidence. ☐

A statement that the practitioner feels a true and fair view is given. ☐

A statement that the practitioner does not feel a true and fair view is given. ☐

Task 5

Fish Tales is a seafood restaurant. Customers pay by cash or bank card. There is an automatic link for bank card payments so that the amount is automatically transferred into the company's bank account. Most payments are made by bank card. Purchases are made on credit. There is a large payroll of cooking and waiting staff. The restaurant rents its premises. Its kitchen equipment, which it owns is old and low value.

Identify which of the following accounting systems are likely to be subject to external audit procedures.

	Likely to be subject to audit procedures	Not likely to be subject to audit procedures
Sales	☐	☐
Payables	☐	☐
Non-current assets	☐	☐

Task 6

The external auditor assesses control risk in order to determine the audit approach.

Identify whether the following factors are likely to lead to the auditor assessing that there is an increase or a decrease in control risk, by selecting the appropriate option.

The company has an internal audit function.	▼
The staff in the accounts department have all worked in their positions for a very long time.	▼
There is a new managing director at the company who is impatient of control restraints.	▼

Picklist:

Increase
Decrease

Task 7

An entity uses internal control procedures in order to mitigate risks to which the entity is exposed. Listed below are two risks that exist in the sales system.

Match each internal control procedure with the risk it is designed to mitigate, by completing the table with the appropriate procedure for each risk.

Risk	Internal control procedure to mitigate
Customer has a poor credit rating	
Goods despatched but not invoiced	

Picklist:

Credit checks prior to accepting custom
Customer's existing balance checked prior to acceptance of order
Goods despatch notes matched with invoice
Goods outwards checked for quality

Task 8

The following are descriptions of procedures within the purchases system of Brunswick Ltd.

Identify whether each of the following procedures is a strength or a weakness of that system by selecting the appropriate option.

John inspects all goods inwards, filing the delivery note in the production office. No other procedures are performed.		▼
Supplier statements are sent to Sandra, who reconciles them with the purchase ledger.		▼

Picklist:

Strength
Weakness

Task 9

Kitchwood Ltd has had to respond to a new competitor in its market in the year to 31 March 20X5. Some extracts from the statement profit and loss are as follows:

	20X5 £	20X4 £
Sales revenue	3,453,676	3,579,439
Gross margin	38%	40%
Advertising	31,885	23,689

Which TWO of the following may provide a plausible explanation for movements in Kitchwood's statement of profit and loss?

Increased spending on advertising has caused gross margin to fall.

A high margin product became obsolete during the year.

20X4 sales included a large one-off sale at a lower margin.

There was a cut off error at the end of 20X4 and next year sales were included wrongly.

Task 10

When selecting items in order to perform audit tests, the auditor must ensure that every sampling unit in the population has a chance of being selected. There are some common methods of selecting a sample, described below.

Using the drop down menu, identify which method is described in each case.

The auditor uses a computer program or table to select the sample.	▼
The auditor uses a value-weighted selection.	▼
The auditor uses no structured technique.	▼

Picklist:

Random numbers
Haphazard selection
Interval sampling
Money Unit Sampling

Task 11

Auditors use tests of control and substantive procedures to gather audit evidence.

Identify, for each of the following procedures, whether it is a test of control or a substantive procedure, by selecting the appropriate option.

	Test of control	Substantive procedure
Review of budgets prepared by the company	☐	☐
Vouching of a payment listed on a bank reconciliation to the bank statement	☐	☐
Observation of staff carrying out the inventory count	☐	☐

Task 12

You are carrying out work on the audit of finished goods at Kirke Ltd. Kirke Ltd purchases a variety of metal and plastic components, from which it makes chairs. All the chairs made use the same components and basic production processes, they should all take the same time to make. Kirke therefore applies a standard cost for labour and overheads, which you have already concluded is reasonable. The major factory overhead is electricity. You have selected a sample of ten items of finished goods, with a completed cost of £6.49.

Identify, from the list below, three items the valuation of these finished goods should be verified against to ensure that valuation is reasonable.

| |
| |

| |
| |

| |
| |

Picklist:

Payroll
Pre year end purchase invoice
Post year end purchase invoice
Standard cost card
Pre year end sales invoice
Post year end sales invoice
Electricity invoice
Payslip

Task 13

During the year, Bells Ltd built itself a new head office. The company took out a bank loan to finance the construction. Interest on the loan is charged at 3%. The company has retained a file of invoices relating to the construction. A specific labour team was used, and hours recorded on the job have also been recorded.

Set out, in a manner suitable for inclusion in the audit plan:

(i) **The risks relating to the new head office**

(ii) **The procedures to be undertaken to ensure that the building is properly valued in the financial statements**

Task 14

Auditors use a variety of procedures to obtain evidence.

From the descriptions below, using the drop menu, identify the type of procedure being described.

Reviewing a purchase invoice to confirm the valuation of a non current asset.	▼
Recalculating the depreciation charge.	▼
Writing to customers to ask them about the balance they owe the company.	▼

Picklist: (Reviewing a purchase invoice to confirm the valuation of a non current asset.)

Inspection
Observation

Picklist: (Recalculating the depreciation charge.)

Recalculation
Reperformance

Picklist: (Writing to customers to ask them about the balance they owe the company)

External confirmation
Inquiry

Task 15

Identify whether each of the following statements, in respect of computer assisted audit techniques (CAATs)is true or false by selecting the appropriate option.

	True	False
Auditors can use CAATs to select samples.	☐	☐
Auditors can use CAATs to test controls inherent in computer applications, for example, controls over invoices input to the sales ledger.	☐	☐
Auditors should never input false invoices to a client's system when using CAATs.	☐	☐

Task 16

Identify whether the following statements relating to the control environment of a company are true or false by selecting the appropriate option.

If an auditor assesses that a control environment is strong, he must exercise professional scepticism.	▼
If an auditor assesses that a control environment is weak he must exercise professional scepticism.	▼
It is not possible for an individual to perpetrate a fraud when the control environment is strong and auditors exercise professional scepticism.	▼

Picklist:

True
False

Task 17

External auditors use a variety of different types of working paper to ascertain systems.

Match the following descriptions to the type of working paper, using drag and drop from the pick list below.

A list of questions designed to give reasonable assurance of effective internal control within a given transactions cycle.	
A picture of the system using symbols with limited narrative.	
A list of controls expected to exist within a system.	

Picklist:

Checklist
ICQ
Narrative notes
Automated working paper
Flowchart
Audit strategy

Task 18

Which of the following reasons audit working papers are prepared is the most important?

- Assisting the audit team to plan and perform the audit ☐
- Creating a record of the audit work carried out to support the audit opinion ☐
- Retaining a record of matters of continuing significance ☐
- Enabling external inspections if necessary (for example, by the FRC) ☐

Task 19

The audit team have extracted a list of balances on the sales ledger that were more than 90 days old at the year end (30 September) and that were still outstanding two months later. The following table gives information relating to these receivables.

£28,000 Nassers Ltd	Credit note issued 30 November.
£4,000 Mustapha Ltd	Customer takes on average 120 days to pay balance.
£60,000 Jasmine Ltd	Cash receipt covering balance in full received December 31st.
£750 Alladin Ltd	Credit note issued 1 January.

Which of the following values is the appropriate value that should be included in the financial statements in respect of these receivables?

- £92,750 ☐
- £64,000 ☐
- £60,000 ☐
- £28,750 ☐

Task 20

You are planning the tests of detail over the payroll at Vance Ltd, to verify the assertions occurrence, measurement and completeness. The payroll is produced by Annie, who obtains monthly clockcards from the production manager, inputs the hours into her computer package which contains all the other relevant details from the employee files, and runs the payroll. It is taken to a director for approval before electronic payments are made to employees. Sample size has been set at six.

Set out, in a manner suitable for inclusion in the audit plan, the audit tests to be carried out on payroll. You are not required to set out tests relating to leavers and joiners.

Task 21

During the audit of Birch Ltd, the audit junior identified that the owner-director of Fasterfoods Ltd, a supplier of foods to restaurants, often took goods home for his own use without noting what he had taken.

In respect of this matter, select whether the audit junior should take no further action or refer to the supervisor.	▼

Picklist:

No further action
Refer to supervisor

Task 22

During the audit of Rocksteady Ltd, the audit junior discovered two instances of the client staff misfiling sales invoices. He reviewed the records and found no evidence of the transactions having been input wrongly.

In respect of this matter, select whether the audit junior should take no further action or refer to the supervisor.	▼

Picklist:

No further action
Refer to supervisor

··

Task 23

During the audit of Beaper Ltd, a new client, it was discovered that the company does not maintain inventory records. Peter Veales is in charge of inventory. He issues inventory to production staff when requested, and reorders when inventory seems low. Levels of inventory are monitored annually, when the company carries out its inventory count.

Prepare extracts, suitable for inclusion in a report to management of Beaper Ltd, which set out:

(i) **The possible consequences in respect of this matter, and**

(ii) **The recommendations that you would make**

··

Task 24

Identify, for each of the following situations which have arisen in two unrelated audit clients, whether or not they will impact the audit report on the financial statements.

	Impact	No impact
Tombli Ltd has a large debt due from Boo Ltd, which the directors believe to be in doubt. The directors have informed the auditors that they believe this debt is not recoverable and have written down its value in the financial statements.	☐	☐
There is significant uncertainty relating to the going concern assumption at Daisy Ltd. The directors have disclosed the uncertainty, which is significant, in the notes to the financial statements.	☐	☐

Task 25

For each of the following situations which have arisen in two unrelated audit clients, select whether or not the audit report on the financial statements would be modified.

Delta Ltd has a large debt due from Zeta Ltd, which the auditors believe to be in doubt. The directors disagree with the auditors, but have made the amendments in the financial statements the auditors believe necessary.	▼
There is significant uncertainty relating to the outcome of a tribunal case that Gamma Ltd is involved in, and has been since before the year end. An employee is suing the company for disability discrimination, and if his case were found in his favour, the compensation could be material to Gamma Ltd.	▼

Picklist:

Modified
Not modified

Task 26

During the audit of Clouds Ltd, the audit junior was asked by a senior member of staff if he could disclose to him the salary levels of other senior ranking members of staff.

Which ONE of the following is NOT an appropriate action for the audit junior to take?

Disclosing the information ☐

Discussing the matter with the audit senior before talking again to the senior staff member ☐

Reporting the matter to the audit partner directly ☐

Ringing the ethical helpline of his professional body for advice ☐

Task 27

Identify whether each of the following audit objectives is a legal requirement in the UK by selecting the appropriate option.

	Legal requirement	Not a legal requirement
Obtain reasonable assurance that the financial statements are free from material misstatement	☐	☐
Give an opinion as to whether the financial statements give a true and fair view	☐	☐
Maintain professional scepticism when planning and performing the audit	☐	☐

Task 28

Identify whether the following statements in respect of external auditor's liability limitation are true or false, by selecting the appropriate option.

Auditors can negotiate a limited liability agreement with clients so that they are not liable for damages above certain preagreed limits.	▾
Audit firms can function as Limited Liability Partnerships which means that partners' personal liability is restricted in the same way as a company shareholder's, but the audit firm may still be liable to clients for negligence.	▾

Picklist:

True
False

Task 29

Which ONE of the following is most accurate in describing the role of international standards on auditing in promoting audit?

The International Audit and Assurance Standards Board issues standards, including quality control standards and members are encouraged to adopt them. ☐

The International Audit and Assurance Standards Board issues standards, including quality control standards and members are required to adopt them. ☐

The International Audit and Assurance Standards Board has issued an International Quality Control Standard which is compulsory for all audit firms to adopt before undertaking audit work. ☐

UK audit firms are required to follow international standards on auditing issued by the International Audit and Assurance Standards Board. ☐

Task 30

When planning an audit of financial statements, the external auditor is required to assess the risks of material misstatement arising in the financial statements.

Identify which component of audit risk the following represent, by selecting the appropriate option.

The company has a high number of cash sales.	▼
A one man operation has recently expanded and taken on staff, and the structures and operating practices have not yet been analysed and formalised.	▼
The directors all have profit related bonuses.	▼

Picklist:

Inherent
Control
Detection

Task 31

Which ONE of the following is a valid definition of materiality?

5% of profit before tax ☐

Measure of the significance of an item to readers ☐

Amount set by auditors as less than materiality for the whole financial statement ☐

Chance of the auditors drawing an incorrect audit conclusion ☐

Task 32

Interviewing and listening skills are important tools for an auditor in applying professional scepticism when interviewing a client.

The managing director of Zhenshi Ltd stated to the audit senior in the course of a meeting that the company had complied with all relevant laws and regulations in the course of its business during the year. However, subsequently, the auditor saw a reference in the board minutes to the fine that the company had to pay the regulator in respect of some minor breaches during the year.

Complete the following statement in respect of the auditor's attitude to any further statements made by the managing director, by selecting the appropriate option.

Further statements made by the managing director in the course of the audit should be

Picklist:

Relied upon without question
Corroborated with other evidence as far as possible

BPP PRACTICE ASSESSMENT 2
EXTERNAL AUDITING

ANSWERS

External auditing

Task 1

	Likely	Unlikely
Lizbet Ltd has been a client for two years. After the previous two audits, the firm raised control issues with the client in a report to management, and the recommendations were implemented. The directors are keen to improve the company's operations. The audit team has not relied on controls in the previous audits.	✓ – reliance on controls is an efficient audit method. There is a good control environment and improved controls.	☐
Mattieu Ltd is a new client. An audit team has ascertained its controls system, which is extensive, and have been given access to the internal audit department's most recent report on controls.	✓ – there is a significant control system, and evidence of monitoring and improvement.	☐
Emilie Ltd is an established client. The managing director is closely involved in all key aspects of the business and favours getting things done over following the book.	☐	✓ – weak control environment.

Task 2

Company pays the correct employees	Control objective	▼
Company pays the incorrect employees	Risk	▼
Company checks pay against budgets	Control procedure	▼

Task 3

Lack of an internal audit function to monitor the controls ☑

Task 4

A statement that nothing has come to the practitioner's attention to indicate that a true and fair view is not given. ☑

Task 5

	Likely to be subject to audit procedures	Not likely to be subject to audit procedures
Sales	☑	☐
Payables	☑	☐
Non-current assets	☐	☑

Task 6

The company has an internal audit function.	Decrease ▼
The staff in the accounts department have all worked in their positions for a very long time.	Decrease ▼
There is a new managing director at the company who is impatient of control restraints.	Increase ▼

Task 7

Risk	Internal control procedure to mitigate
Customer has a poor credit rating	Credit checks prior to accepting custom
Goods despatched but not invoiced	Goods despatch notes matched with invoice

Task 8

John inspects all goods inwards, filing the delivery note in the production office.	Weakness ▼ – delivery information is not matched with invoice
Supplier statements are sent to Sandra, who reconciles them with the purchase ledger.	Strength ▼

Task 9

A high margin product became obsolete during the year. ☑

There was a cut off error at the end of 20X4 and next year sales were included wrongly. ☑

Task 10

The auditor uses a computer programme or table to select the sample.	Random numbers ▼
The auditor uses a value-weighted selection.	Money Unit Sampling ▼
The auditor uses no structured technique.	Haphazard selection ▼

Task 11

	Test of control	Substantive procedure
Review of budgets prepared by the company	✓ – if the auditor were comparing to actual or to prior year budgets it might be a substantive procedure but in isolation it is a test that the control of preparing budgets exists.	☐
Vouching of a payment listed on a bank reconciliation to the bank statement	☐	✓
Observation of staff carrying out the inventory count	✓	☐

Task 12

Pre year end purchase invoice – to ensure that raw material cost is reflected correctly in finished cost

Standard cost card – to ensure that labour and overhead cost is reflected correctly in finished cost (you have already tested the validity of standard costs)

Post year end sales invoice – to ensure that net realisable value is not higher than finished cost

Task 13

Risks

- The building may not be valued correctly in the financial statements for various reasons:
    - Costs may have been omitted from the valuation
    - Bank interest may have been omitted from the valuation or capitalised incorrectly
    - The valuation might include elements of profit, that would usually be charged to customers

Procedures

- Obtain the valuation calculation
- Verify material costs to invoices

- Verify labour costs to timesheets and payroll
- Ensure no element of profit included in these elements of cost
- Review invoices allocated to valuation to ensure reasonable to capitalise these costs
- Verify capitalised bank interest to bank statements

Note: based on the information available at the time this book was written, we anticipate a task like this would be human marked in the real assessment.

Task 14

Reviewing a purchase invoice to confirm the valuation of a non current asset.	Inspection	▼
Recalculating the depreciation charge.	Recalculation	▼
Writing to customers to ask them about the balance they owe the company.	External confirmation	▼

Task 15

	True	False
Auditors can use CAATs to select samples.	✓	☐
Auditors can use CAATs to test controls inherent in computer applications, for example, controls over invoices input to the sales ledger.	✓	☐
Auditors should never input false invoices to a client's system when using CAATs.	☐	✓

Task 16

If an audit assesses that a control environment is strong, he must exercise professional scepticism.	True	▼
If an audit assesses that a control environment is weak he must exercise professional scepticism.	True	▼
It is not possible for an individual to perpetrate a fraud when the control environment is strong and auditors exercise professional scepticism.	False	▼

Task 17

A list of questions designed to give reasonable assurance of effective internal control within a given transactions cycle.	ICQ
A picture of the system using symbols with limited narrative.	Flowchart
A list of controls expected to exist within a system.	Checklist

Task 18

Creating a record of the audit work carried out to support the audit opinion ✓

Task 19

£64,000 ✓

The items that have been credited after date should not be included in the year end total.

Task 20

Payroll

1. Select six payroll entries from across the year (suggest one every two months)
2. Confirm pay rates/tax rates/deductions to employee files
3. Confirm hours worked to monthly clockcard
4. Confirm calculations inherent in payroll (net pay, deductions, gross pay)
5. Confirm deductions (NI, PAYE and any pension/other) have been made correctly
6. Trace net pay to bank payment records
7. Ensure payroll authorised by senior official
8. Agree payment to bank statement/cash book

Note: based on the information available at the time this book was written, we anticipate a task like this would be human marked in the real assessment.

Task 21

In respect of this matter, select whether the audit junior should take no further action or refer to the supervisor.	Refer to supervisor ▼

Task 22

In respect of this matter, select whether the audit junior should take no further action or refer to the supervisor.	No further action ▼

Task 23

Consequences

- Inventory is issued to production staff when requested, so there is a risk that inventory may be used inefficiently in production – with no records to show how much was used on a particular job there is no control over how efficiently the company operates

- As inventory is only monitored annually, it is at risk of being subject to theft – there is little to stop Peter defrauding the company by taking goods for personal use

- With no planning of the use of inventory, and Peter repurchasing when things seem low, there is a risk that goods will be unavailable when required for use in the business

Recommendations

- Inventory use should be better planned so that inventory is always available when required – re order levels should be set based on normal usage, and requisitions made when unusual usage is anticipated

- Inventory movements to production could be recorded, and possibly allocated to job number which records could be reviewed to ensure that inventory is used in an efficient manner

Note: based on the information available at the time this book was written, we anticipate a task like this would be human marked in the real assessment.

Task 24

	Impact	No impact
Tombli Ltd has a large debt due from Boo Ltd, which the directors believe to be in doubt. The directors have informed the auditors that they believe this debt is not recoverable and have written down its value in the financial statements.		✓
There is significant uncertainty relating to the going concern assumption at Daisy Ltd. The directors have disclosed the uncertainty, which is significant, in the notes to the financial statements..	✓ An emphasis of matter paragraph will be included	

Task 25

Delta Ltd has a large debt due from Zeta Ltd, which the auditors believe to be in doubt. The directors disagree with the auditors, but have made the amendments in the financial statements the auditors believe necessary.	Not modified ▼ – as the directors have made the appropriate changes, the opinion will be unqualified.
There is significant uncertainty relating to the outcome of a tribunal case that Gamma Ltd is involved in, and has been since before the year end. An employee is suing the company for disability discrimination, and if his case were found in his favour, the compensation could be material to Gamma Ltd.	Modified ▼ – whatever action the directors take about this matter, the auditors will issue a modified **report**, as they will emphasise the matter in a special paragraph. Whether the opinion is modified or not, depends on how the directors have disclosed the matter in the financial statements.

Task 26

Disclosing the information ✓

It would be inappropriate for him to disclose this confidential information to the staff member. It would not be wrong for him to ring the ethical helpline, but it would probably be unnecessary – as it would be best for him to seek advice from other members of the audit team first.

Task 27

	Legal requirement	Not a legal requirement
Obtain reasonable assurance that the financial statements are free from material misstatement	☐	✓
Give an opinion as to whether the financial statements give a true and fair view	✓	☐
Maintain professional scepticism when planning and performing the audit	☐	✓

(Giving an opinion in relation to a true and fair view is a UK legal requirement)

Task 28

Auditors can negotiate a limited liability agreement with clients so that they are not liable for damages above certain preagreed limits.	True ▼
Audit firms can function as Limited Liability Partnerships which means that partners' personal liability is restricted in the same way as a company shareholder's, but the audit firm may still be liable to clients for negligence.	True ▼

Task 29

The International Audit and Assurance Standards Board issues standards, including quality control standards and members are encouraged to adopt them. ✓

Task 30

The company has a high number of cash sales.	Inherent ▼
A one man operation has recently expanded and taken on staff, and the structures and operating practices have not yet been analysed and formalised.	Control ▼
The directors all have profit related bonuses.	Inherent ▼

Task 31

Measure of the significance of an item to readers ✓

Task 32

Further statements made by the managing director in the course of the audit should be

Corroborated with other evidence as far as possible ▼

BPP PRACTICE ASSESSMENT 3
EXTERNAL AUDITING

Time allowed: 2 hours

External auditing

Task 1

The external auditor may seek to place reliance on internal controls in order to restrict substantive testing.

Identify, in each of the following circumstances, whether the external auditor is likely to place reliance, or place no reliance on internal controls, by selecting the appropriate option.

The accounts department at Kadny Ltd consists of one member of staff.	▼
There is good segregation of duties at Tandy Ltd, and controls are monitored by management in each department.	▼
The controls at Landy Ltd sound good when described to the auditor, but they realise through observation that the financial controller regularly overrides controls to achieve objectives.	▼

Picklist:

Reliance
No reliance

Task 2

Accounting systems have control objectives and control procedures to mitigate the risks that the control objective is not met.

Identify, for each of the following, whether they are a control objective, risk or control procedure, by selecting the appropriate option.

A company should only pay the correct suppliers.	▼
A company might pay a supplier twice for the same liability.	▼
A company should never allow blank cheques to be signed.	▼

Picklist:

Control objective
Risk
Control procedure

Task 3

Identify whether the following statements in respect of limitations of internal controls are true or false, by selecting the appropriate option.

The fact that people using the system may make mistakes is not a limitation of internal controls.	▼
The fact that people may collude to override controls and commit a fraud is a limitation of internal controls.	▼
The fact that directors may omit important areas when designing control systems is not a limitation of internal controls.	▼

Picklist:

True
False

Task 4

Which ONE of the following is not a benefit of assurance?

Users of financial statements will have more confidence that they are presented fairly. ☐

Potential fraudsters might be deterred by regular scrutiny of the financial records. ☐

Management might be motivated to operate systems properly by the thought of a regular review of these systems. ☐

Financiers will know the company is financially secure. ☐

Task 5

Makeit Company Ltd is a manufacturing company with a heavy investment in machinery and buildings. It has a large number of staff. Goods are bought and sold on credit.

Which of the following items are most likely to be focused on during the external audit?

Non-current assets, sales revenue, purchases and payroll. ☐

Non-current assets, receivables, payables and payroll. ☐

Investments, receivables, payables and payroll. ☐

Investments, sales revenue, purchases and payroll. ☐

Task 6

The external auditor assesses control risk in order to determine the audit approach.

Identify whether the following factors are likely to lead to the auditor assessing that there is an increase or a decrease in control risk, by selecting the appropriate option.

The financial controller submits detailed budgets to the managing director and scrutinises variances from actual in detail.	▼
The company has a detailed set of control procedures which staff are required to follow.	▼
The directors ensure there is good segregation of duties at the company.	▼

Picklist:

Increase
Decrease

Task 7

An entity uses internal control procedures in order to mitigate the risks to which the entity is exposed. Listed below are two internal control procedures which are applicable to an entity's payroll system.

Identify, for each of the following internal control procedures, the risk that it mitigates, by completing the table with the risk mitigated.

Internal control procedure	Risk mitigated
Personnel records are kept and wages and salaries checked to details held in them.	
The payroll should be approved by someone who has not prepared it.	

Picklist:

The company may overpay its staff

A payroll fraud could be perpetrated

The company might break the law relating to deductions

The bank may turn down the BACS request

Task 8

The following are descriptions of procedures within the non-current assets system of Primrose Ltd.

Identify whether each of the following procedures is a strength or a deficiency.

	Strength	Deficiency
Divisional managers raise procurement orders for new non-current assets, which are approved by the board.	☐	☐
Divisional managers are required to review all non-current assets in their divisions on a monthly basis.	☐	☐

Task 9

The external auditor is required to undertake analytical procedures as part of the planning process in order to identify the risk of misstatement of figures in the financial statements. The auditors have calculated that gross profit percentage has risen from last year, but the sales director has informed them there have been no significant changes in operations, sales levels or sales mix since last year.

Which TWO of the following may provide a plausible explanation for the rise in gross profit?

Sales invoices relating to the next period may have been wrongly included in the current period. ☐

Sales invoices relating to the current period may have been wrongly included in the next period. ☐

Purchase invoices relating to the current period may have been wrongly included in the next period. ☐

Purchase invoices relating to the next period may have been wrongly included in the current period. ☐

Task 10

When selecting items in order to perform tests of detail, the auditor has to consider a number of factors.

Identify, for each of the following factors, the impact they will have on sample size by selecting the appropriate option.

Stratifying the sample by value.	▼
Testing 100% of the population.	▼
Decision to carry out initial analytical procedures on the population.	▼

Picklist:

Increase
Decrease
No effect

....

Task 11

Auditors use tests of control and substantive procedures to gather audit evidence.

Identify whether each of the procedures below is a test of control, an analytical procedure or a test of detail, by selecting the appropriate option.

The auditor is comparing the average salary per the payroll for last year to the average salary per the payroll for this year, taking into account known factors, such as the general 3% pay rise.	▼
The auditor is inspecting a purchase invoice for evidence that Doris, the purchase ledger clerk, checked the calculations on the invoice prior to entering the invoice into the system.	▼
The auditor is inspecting a purchase invoice to vouch the value of an addition to non current assets.	▼

Picklist:

Test of control
Analytical procedure
Test of detail

....

Task 12

An audit junior is going to perform a verification of the bank reconciliation carried out by the company at the year end. The junior has asked for guidance on the work to be performed in respect of this reconciliation.

Match each reconciling item with the piece of evidence the reconciling item should be checked to:

(i)   Cash book balance

(ii) Cheque payments

(iii) Unbanked receipts

(iv) Bank statement balance

Picklist:

Cash book
Pre year end bank statements
Post year end bank statements
Bank letter

Task 13

At 30 June 20X2, Benja Ltd had a trade receivable outstanding from Mina Ltd of £250,000. This is a material debt. Mina Ltd is a long standing customer who has had a history of late payment. The audit senior has performed analytical review on the receivable, and it is 5% higher than last year. Sales revenue to Mina Ltd has not increased in the year.

Identify, for the purposes of the audit plan:

(i)   **The audit risks relating to the overall receivables balance resulting from this outstanding receivable.**

(ii) **The procedures to be taken to ensure that the receivable from Mina Ltd is fairly stated in the financial statements.**

Task 14

When testing transactions and balances, the external auditor will gain assurance about different assertions regarding those transactions and balances.

In respect of the assertions given below, select the information which will provide primary assurance.

Existence of a non current asset	▼
Completeness of payables	▼
Valuation of raw materials	▼

Picklist: (Existence of a non current asset)

The asset itself
An entry in the non current assets register

Picklist: (Completeness of payables)

Supplier statements
Purchase invoices

Picklist: (Valuation of raw material)

Purchase invoice
Inventory records

....

Task 15

Select which Computer Assisted Audit Technique (CAAT) should be used in the following situations.

To help an auditor to select a sample from a large population.	▼
To help an auditor compare large volumes of data from the current and prior year.	▼
To help an auditor test whether application controls are working in a computer programme.	▼

Picklist:

Audit software
Test data

....

Task 16

An external auditor is required to obtain an understanding of the control environment within an audited entity.

Identify whether the following factors contribute to a strong control environment or a weak control environment.

	Strong	Weak
The sales department is very target orientated. Staff and management are appraised solely on sales target achievements.	☐	☐
The company has a dedicated internal audit department whose main role is to monitor adherence to company policies and procedures.	☐	☐

Task 17

External auditors use a variety of methods for documenting systems of control, including flowcharts, internal control questionnaires and narrative notes.

For each of the following definitions, identify the method being described by selecting the appropriate method of documentation.

A list of questions designed to ascertain whether the system has a minimum level of controls to achieve objectives.	▼
A description of the system.	▼

Picklist:

Narrative notes
Flowchart
Internal control questionnaire

Task 18

Identify whether the following statements in respect of what will appear on an external auditor's working papers are true or false by selecting the appropriate option.

The date the work was carried out	▼
The date the work was reviewed by a more senior member of staff than the person who carried out the result	▼
The audit area being tested	▼

Picklist:

True
False

Task 19

At Aristo Ltd, a full year's depreciation is charged in year of purchase. The following depreciation rates apply:

Property:	2% straight line
Plant:	10% straight line
Vehicles:	25% straight line

You are recalculating the depreciation charge shown in the notes to the financial statements for additions, the values of which are as follows:

Cutting machine	£25,000
Car for managing director	£25,000

Identify the appropriate depreciation charge in each case by selecting the appropriate option.

Cutting machine	▼
Car	▼

Picklist:

£0
£2,500
£6,250

Task 20

You are planning the audit of trade payables at Fairycake Ltd. Fairycake is an established client, and the manager has concerns that it is experiencing cashflow difficulties. This is partly because the bank, which has lent Fairycake a considerable sum, has recently specified that it requires Fairycake to maintain an current ratio of 1.5:1 in order to keep its bank funding.

In the past, Fairycake has retained yearend statements from its major suppliers for the auditors to use. This year, the manager has requested that all such statements are retained, although the client has stated that not all suppliers send such statements.

Initial analytical review on purchases suggests that purchases in the last month of the year look low.

Set out, in a manner suitable for inclusion in the audit plan, the audit procedures to be undertaken in order to ensure that the trade payables balance is complete in the financial statements.

Task 21

During the audit of Crocus Ltd (annual revenue £12,000,000) for the year ended 31 December 20X1, when reviewing the cash book, the audit junior identified a monthly round sum payment of £1,000 to a company, entitled 'management charges'. Crocus is a single company with no other related companies.

In respect of this matter, select what action the audit junior should take.	▼

Picklist:

Refer to supervisor
Take no further action

Task 22

During the audit of Tulip Ltd, when reviewing the payroll, the audit junior noticed small number of staff had the same names as superhero characters (for example, Clark Kent and Peter Parker). He was suspicious of this, so requested their personnel files, which he was given. The files contain the same details as other personnel files he has seen. All of these staff work at the other site, which is a great distance from where the audit junior is based.

In respect of this matter, select what the audit junior should do next.	▼

Picklist:

No further action
Refer to supervisor

Task 23

During the audit of Daffs Ltd, a new client, the audit junior established that in the accounts department, Daphne records sales receipts with the receptionist. Daphne then posts receipts to the sales ledger, places the cheques in her desk drawer, which she locks when she is not at her desk. Receipts are all banked together on Friday afternoons.

Prepare extracts, suitable for inclusion in a report to management of Daffs Ltd, which set out

(i)   **The possible consequences of this matter, and**
(ii)   **The recommendations that you would make**

Task 24

ISA 265 *Communicating deficiencies in internal control to those charged with governance and management* defines a significant deficiency in internal control as a deficiency or combination of deficiencies in internal control that, in the auditors professional judgement, is of sufficient importance to merit the attention of those charged with governance.

Identify whether or not the following deficiency in internal control is a significant deficiency by selecting the appropriate option:

The identification of a fraud, relating to an immaterial monetary amount, carried out by employee of the audited entity, due to a control weakness previously communicated to management by the auditors.

▼

Picklist:

Not a significant deficiency
Significant deficiency

....

Task 25

For each of the following situations which have arisen in two unrelated audit clients, select whether or not the audit opinion on the financial statements would be modified.

The directors of Forsyth Ltd have included an optimistic review of the year in their directors' report. The auditors believe that it is inconsistent with the financial statements, and in addition, that some financial analysis in the directors' report has been presented in a misleading fashion.		▼
The directors at Jasmine Ltd prepared cash flow forecasts for the auditors to assess with regard to the going concern assumption. These forecasts covered a period of nine months after the yea rend. The auditors were not able to perform alternative procedures to verify the going concern assumption.		▼

Picklist:

Modified
Not modified

....

Task 26

An audit senior has become involved in legal action related to some audit work he undertook on the audit of Seeker Ltd. The auditor has a duty of confidentiality to Seeker Ltd, but needs to defend himself against allegations that his work was not carried out with due care.

Which ONE of the following is not an appropriate action for the audit senior to take?

Maintain silence, so as not to breach confidentiality. ☐

Obtain advice from his professional body concerning the matter. ☐

Discuss the matter with his legal representation to obtain advice ☐

Disclose what work he did in respect of the matter, and risk
breaching his duty of confidentiality ☐

Task 27

Complete the following statements on the independence of auditors, by selecting the appropriate option in each case..

(a) Auditors should be independent of the company and its directors so that they can give an objective opinion to the [▼]

Picklist:

Directors

Shareholders

(b) Independence can be threatened by [▼], as the auditors can become over-reliant on the client, for instance, due to its fee income.

Picklist:

Self-review

Self-interest

(c) Independence can be threatened by [▼] if the auditors have prepared the financial statements being audited.

Picklist:

Self-review

Intimidation

Task 28

Which ONE of the following is NOT a suitable way for auditors to limit their liability to their clients and other parties?

Disclaimer clause in the auditor's report ☐

Setting up a limited liability partnership ☐

Professional indemnity insurance ☐

Scrutinising every transaction entered by the business ☐

Task 29

Identify whether the following statements in respect of International Standards on Auditing are true or false by selecting the appropriate option.

	True	False
At least half of IAASB's board must approve a draft standard before it is issued as a new International Standard on Auditing.	☐	☐
The IAASB is committed to seeking convergence between international and national standards on auditing to provide high quality auditing on a global basis.	☐	☐

Task 30

Complete the following statements on the risk assessed by auditors by selecting the appropriate options.

(a) [▼] is the risk that the entity's internal control system will not prevent or detect and correct errors.

(b) [▼] is the risk that misstatements will exist in financial statements and the auditors will not discover them.

(c) [▼] is the risk that items will be misstated due to their nature or due to their context.

Picklist:

Audit risk
Inherent risk
Control risk
Detection risk

Task 31

Identify whether the following misstatements are likely to be considered material or not material by external auditors.

	Material	Not material
A condition of Jocey Ltd's loan finance is that profits cover interest on the loans three times. The auditors have discovered a miscalculation in depreciation that increases depreciation by £200, dropping the interest cover to 2.9 times.	☐	☐
During the audit of Kaseys Ltd, the auditors consider that an error equal to 5% of profit or more is material. The auditors have just confirmed that a debt of £25,000 owed by a customer is irrecoverable. Profit is £550,000.	☐	☐

Task 32

Interviewing and listening skills are important tools for an auditor in applying professional scepticism when interviewing a client.

In a meeting with the audit senior, the financial controller of Verity Ltd argued that his interpretation of an accounting standard was just as reasonable as the audit senior's and that he was unwilling to amend the accounts. However, later, when the Finance Director joined the discussion, he agreed with the auditor's interpretation of the accounting standard.

Identify whether or not other assertions made by the financial controller will be considered less reliable or not by the auditor as a result of these discussions, by selecting the appropriate option.

	Less reliable	Not less reliable
The auditor will consider other assertions made by the financial controller to be…	☐	☐

BPP PRACTICE ASSESSMENT 3
EXTERNAL AUDITING

ANSWERS

External auditing

Task 1

The accounts department at Kadny Ltd consists of one member of staff.	No reliance	▼
There is good segregation of duties at Tandy Ltd, and controls are monitored by management in each department.	Reliance	▼
The controls at Landy Ltd sound good when described to the auditor, but they realise through observation that the financial controller regularly overrides controls to achieve objectives.	No reliance	▼

Task 2

A company should only pay the correct suppliers.	Control objective	▼
A company might pay a supplier twice for the same liability.	Risk	▼
A company should never allow blank cheques to be signed.	Control procedure	▼

Task 3

The fact that people using the system may make mistakes is not a limitation of internal controls.	False	▼
The fact that people may collude to override controls and commit a fraud is a limitation of internal controls.	True	▼
The fact that directors may omit important areas when designing control systems is not a limitation of internal controls.	False	▼

Task 4

Financiers will know the company is financially secure. ☑

Task 5

Non-current assets, receivables, payables and payroll ☑

Task 6

The financial controller submits detailed budgets to the managing director and scrutinises variances from actual in detail.	Decrease	▼
The company has a detailed set of control procedures which staff are required to follow.	Decrease	▼
The directors ensure there is good segregation of duties at the company.	Decrease	▼

Task 7

Internal control procedure	Risk mitigated
Personnel records are kept and wages and salaries checked to details held in them.	The company may overpay its staff
The payroll should be approved by someone who has not prepared it.	A payroll fraud could be perpetrated

---

Task 8

	Strength	Deficiency
Divisional managers raise procurement orders for new non-current assets, which are approved by the board.	☑ – purchases are authorised	☐
Divisional managers are required to review all non-current assets in their divisions on a monthly basis.	☑ – the company ensures it assets are maintained properly	☐

Task 9

Sales invoices relating to the next period may have been wrongly included in the current period. ☑

Purchase invoices relating to the current period may have been wrongly included in the next period. ☑

....

Task 10

Stratifying the sample by value.	Decrease	▼
Testing 100% of the population.	Increase	▼
Decision to carry out initial analytical procedures on the population.	Decrease	▼

....

Task 11

The auditor is comparing the average salary per the payroll for last year to the average salary per the payroll for this year, taking into account known factors, such as the general 3% pay rise.	Analytical procedure	▼
The auditor is inspecting a purchase invoice for evidence that Doris, the purchase ledger clerk, checked the calculations on the invoice prior to entering the invoice into the system.	Test of control	▼
The auditor is inspecting a purchase invoice to vouch the value of an addition to non current assets.	Test of detail	▼

....

Task 12

(i)	Cash book balance	Cash book
(ii)	Cheque payments	Post year end bank statements
(iii)	Unbanked receipts	Post year end bank statements
(iv)	Bank statement balance	Bank letter

....

Task 13

Note: based on the information available at the time this book was written, we anticipate a task like this would be human marked in the real assessment.

(i) Audit risks

- There is a risk that the receivable contains an element which Mina Ltd does not intend, or can't afford, to pay.
- There is a risk that Mina Ltd is in financial difficulties and the whole amount will become irrecoverable.

(ii) Procedures

- Request that the client request confirmation from Mina Ltd that it intends to pay the balance (confirmation should be sent direct to auditors).
- Scrutinise reply from Mina Ltd and draw audit conclusions about the recoverability of the balance.

In addition, or instead if Mina Ltd does not reply after prompting

- Obtain an aged analysis of Mina's balance.
- Scrutinise aged analysis for any old balances that have not been paid, and analyse the payment pattern on the account (are older amounts paid in advance of newer invoices?)
- Review payments after date (if any) and compare to age analysis
- Discuss audit findings with credit controller to assess whether he has any relevant additional information about Mina's outstanding balance.

Task 14

Existence of a non current asset	The asset itself ▼
Completeness of payables	Supplier statements ▼
Valuation of raw materials	Purchase invoice ▼

Task 15

To help an auditor to select a sample from a large population.	Audit software ▼
To help an auditor compare large volumes of data from the current and prior year.	Audit software ▼
To help an auditor test whether application controls are working in a computer programme.	Test data ▼

Task 16

	Strong	Weak
The sales department is very target orientated. Staff and management are appraised solely on sales target achievements.	☐	☑
The company has a dedicated internal audit department whose main role is to monitor adherence to company policies and procedures.	☑	☐

Task 17

A list of questions designed to ascertain whether the system has a minimum level of controls to achieve objectives.	Internal control questionnaire	▼
A description of the system.	Narrative notes	▼

Task 18

The date the work was carried out	True	▼
The date the work was reviewed by a more senior member of staff than the person who carried out the result	True	▼
The audit area being tested	True	▼

Task 19

Cutting machine	£2,500	▼
Car	£6,250	▼

Task 20

Note: based on the information available at the time this book was written, we anticipate a task like this would be human marked in the real assessment.

- Select a sample of payables balances to verify. As payables has been determined to be risky this year, this sample will be higher than in previous years. It should include all material items at the yearend and a representative sample from the rest, perhaps selected systematically so as to avoid bias to high value items.

- Obtain supplier statements for the sampled items, and reconcile the purchase ledger balances to the supplier statements. Particular attention should be paid to Invoices from the last month of the year, which Fairycake may have (wrongly) deferred into the next year.

- If supplier statements are not available for sampled items, consider whether alternative procedures provide sufficient evidence (such as scrutinising purchase invoices on the account). This will depend in part on the strength of purchase controls, and in part on the results of supplier statement reconciliations. If invoices appear to have been routinely deferred, it may be necessary to circularise suppliers from whom no statements are available.

- Perform a review of goods received notes in the last week of the year, and ensure that related invoices have been processed in the correct period. If it appears invoices have been deliberated deferred, this test may need to be extended to earlier in the month.

Task 21

In respect of this matter, select what action the audit junior should take.	Refer to supervisor ▼ – although the total amount transferred is immaterial, it is a round sum payment that has no obvious rationale – why would an unconnected company be paying management charges?

Task 22

In respect of this matter, select what the audit junior should do next.	Refer to supervisor – this could be legitimate, but could also be a payroll fraud, in which case the personnel files could have been invented as well. The supervisor might deem it necessary to identify one of the staff members at the other site, particularly if the sums involved for the superheroes salaries is material.

Task 23

(i)   Consequences

- Daphne's desk drawer does not seem to be a suitably secure place to store cash receipts, even if it sometimes locked. There is a significant risk that these receipts could be stolen or lost. In an extreme case, if the desk was affected by fire, the desk drawer is unlikely to be fireproof, and the cheques could be destroyed.

- Receipts are only banked once a week, which exposes the company to the threat of their loss, and also the loss of potential interest on those receipts for the days that the receipts are owned but not cashed, or the lack of cash powering the business because it is in a desk drawer.

(ii)   Recommendations

- The company should invest in a safe so that receipts can be kept more securely when they have not yet been banked.

- Daphne should bank receipts more frequently, ideally daily, which would convert the cheques to cash more quickly and also reduce the risk of loss.

- In the long term, Daffs should consider asking customers to pay their balances by electronic transfer direct to their bank account, which would speed up the process of cash conversion further, and would eliminate the risk of loss of cash receipts.

Note: based on the information available at the time this book was written, we anticipate a task like this would be human marked in the real assessment.

Task 24

The identification of a fraud, relating to an immaterial monetary amount, carried out by employee of the audited entity, due to a control weakness previously communicated to management by the auditors.

Significant deficiency ▼

Task 25

The directors of Forsyth Ltd have included an optimistic review of the year in their directors' report. The auditors believe that it is inconsistent with the financial statements, and in addition, that some financial analysis in the directors' report has been presented in a misleading fashion.	Modified ▼ – the auditors cannot conclude that the directors' report agrees with the financial statements.
The directors at Jasmine Ltd prepared cash flow forecasts for the auditors to assess with regard to the going concern assumption. These forecasts covered a period of nine months after the year end. They would not extend them The auditors were not able to perform alternative procedures to verify the going concern assumption.	Modified ▼ – this represents a limitation of scope on the audit, as the auditors would expect to see at least twelve months.

Task 26

Maintain silence, so as not to breach confidentiality. ☑
The auditor is entitled to defend himself in a legal situation. Seeking advice from his solicitor and professional body are also acceptable.

Task 27

(a) Auditors should be independent of the company and its directors so that they can give an objective opinion to the | **shareholders**.▼ |

(b) Independence can be threatened by | **self-interest** ▼ | , as the auditors can become over-reliant on the client, for instance, due to its fee income,

(c) Independence can be threatened by | **self-review** ▼ | if the auditors have prepared the financial statements being audited.

Task 28

Scrutinising every transaction entered by the business ☑

This would not guarantee a correct audit decision anyway, and would mean that the audit firm would surely go out of business, as their fees would be too high to compete with other firms.

Task 29

	True	False
At least half of IAASB's board must approve a draft standard before it is issued as a new International Standards on Auditing.	☐	☑ – in fact 2/3rds must approve it.
The IAASB is committed to seeking convergence between international and national standards on auditing to provide high quality auditing on a global basis.	☑	☐

Task 30

(a) | Control risk ▼ | is the risk that the entity's internal control system will not prevent or detect and correct errors

(b) | Detection risk ▼ | is the risk that misstatements will exist in financial statements and the auditors will not discover them.

(c) | Inherent risk ▼ | is the risk that items will be misstated due to their nature or due to their context.

Task 31

	Material	Not material
A condition of Jocey Ltd's loan finance is that profits cover interest on the loans three times. The auditors have discovered a miscalculation in depreciation that increases depreciation by £200, dropping the interest cover to 2.9 times.	✓	☐
During the audit of Kaseys Ltd, the auditors consider that an error equal to 5% of profit or more is material. The auditors have just confirmed that a debt of £25,000 owed by a customer is irrecoverable. Profit is £550,000.	☐	✓

Task 32

	Less reliable	Not less reliable
The auditor will consider other assertions made by the financial controller to be…	☐	✓

Notes

Notes

Notes